# The Horses In Our Stars

# The Horses In Our Stars

## A Story of Life, Love, and the Journey Within

Chris Lombard

With A Foreword By Kevin Hancock

Author of *Not For Sale:*
*Finding Center in the Land of Crazy Horse*

MILL CITY PRESS

Mill City Press, Inc.
2301 Lucien Way #415
Maitland, FL 32751
407.339.4217
www.millcitypress.net

Printed in the United States of America

ISBN-13: 978-1-54566-197-0

For those who have walked with me
and for the love we shared

# Table of Contents

# Foreword

What's this book about?

My favorite stories cause the reader (and sometimes even the author) to pause before answering this seemingly fundamental question.

I first met Chris Lombard in 2018 as we sat in a small conference room inside the Hancock Lumber store in Windham, Maine. We had each spent a good part of a decade answering an inner calling that led us from New England to the American West. Both of us were searching, and both of us were following, neither fully understanding what had brought us there, nor what gifts—if any—the odyssey would impart.

For Chris, the journey gave birth to a deeply spiritual relationship with the horse. At age twenty-six, when he first traveled west, Chris was just learning about horses. Today, he is one of the most adept horsemen in America.

For me, a single trip to the remote and traditionally recalcitrant Pine Ridge Indian Reservation changed my view of myself and, therefore, my relationship to the world. I have now been to the reservation sixteen times, and the lessons I've learned there have changed my life.

Although Chris and I have met face-to-face only once, we understand each other completely.

This book, to me, is about the deep love that comes from embracing the oneness of the Universe. The Lakota call it *Mitakuye Oyasin*, which means all that exists is connected and related. Separateness is an illusion. We are all brothers and sisters.

Deep truths are fundamental to both spirituality and science. Earth is a closed system; nothing gets in or out but sunlight. All that exists originates from the same source. To truly love one person, one horse, one dog, or one flower is the equivalent of loving all people, all horses, all dogs, and all flowers. "I am in love with it all," Chris writes toward the end of this elixir of a story.

But how does one come to this foundational yet translucent awareness? And what does one do with this knowledge, once acquired, in a world consumed by the 24/7 viewing and sharing of life through a phone?

This beautiful book, *The Horses in Our Stars*, answers both questions.

"It starts with finding a feeling of where you are yourself," Chris writes. Counterintuitive as it may seem, to feel the connectivity that surrounds us, we first must explore the darkness and the light within ourselves.

In 2010, I acquired a rare voice disorder called spasmodic dysphonia that often makes speaking difficult. In 2012, I began traveling to Pine Ridge, where I encountered an entire community that did not feel heard. There are lots of ways to lose your voice in this world, I concluded.

Finding one's authentic voice and releasing it to the world is an act of true love, and perhaps even the purpose of a life on Earth. The quest to both honor and transcend the time and place of our birth and self-actualize is central to the human experience. For the rider and the horse to become as one, the rider must work first—and hardest—on himself, and then serve—not master—the horse. This is but one of the levels of transformative awareness Chris acquires, and then shares with his readers.

What changes when we enter this state of awareness and being?

Everything. Paradigms that have stood for centuries are turned inside out.

"In the old ways of horsemanship, it was just about how to get the horse's body to do what we wanted—for travel, for pulling, for farming, for wars," Chris writes. "Physical and mental dominance, solely for our own benefit."

Chris pushes past this view, urging his readers to follow a heightened social path, based on the knowledge that the rider and horse are spiritual equals and fundamentally the same, with neither destined to govern the other: "There's a place we can get to where the horse has freedom to make its own choices. A place where they choose to follow our guidance. Where they get as much out of the relationship as we do," he writes.

In nature, power is dispersed. There is no capital of the desert, no king of the forest. It is the destiny of humanity to reunite with this innate truth.

It's fitting that Chris has acquired the core wisdom that will come to define the Aquarian Age, where everyone is related—every plant, animal, and flower, connected. We humans live in that continuum, not above it.

As such, the rider becomes exceptional only by first finding unconditional love within himself, and then transferring that love to the horse. The rider, who could be master, thus learns to embrace restraint. The horse reciprocates, becoming an inspired participant of its own free will. This is how relationships in the Aquarian Age shall be defined. And, as Chris imparts, it is the only way a horse and human become "some greater single thing uniting both souls as one."

My dear friend Gabrielle LaChiara is a healer and spiritualist. One of her favorite mantras is something I say to myself each day:

> *Love is the cure.*
> *I am love.*
> *I am the cure.*

What's this book about?

It's about love. The kind of love that comes from within, and unveils a connection to all the world.

Kevin Hancock
January 2019

# The Horses In Our Stars

# Prologue

*This is not about me.*

*This is about us.*

*I once stood in a snow covered field in the cold winter when the sun had not been out for days. A somber sky loomed above while fearless winds conjured wisps of snow up and into the air and whirled them across the land like ghosts caught in the ancient rhythms of life.*

*I looked at the openness around me and could not move. An unseen power held me and urged me to take notice. My breathing slowed, the way it always does in such moments. I looked at the pine tree boughs gently holding the snow resting upon them. I could see a lonely line of deer tracks left on a hill. I listened and the winter land quieted. And then this is what happened.*

*The snow began to glow. I strained to keep watching, it was like oncoming headlights shining into my eyes. It got brighter and brighter, and then a wave of cozy warmth came over my body. I was engulfed in the glow and made part of it.*

*It was the sun. It was bursting through the gray sky like a gentle madman, politely tearing away at the clouds, cooped up for too long and now showing itself in all its brilliance in the reflection off the snow.*

*You were there. You saw what I saw, felt the warmth of the sun, and came alive with me. You have felt it many times and in many places. When you laugh. When you dance. When you are in those dreams. There are many such times in this grand adventure. All with those cold, dark, stormy times when the sun has not shone for days.*

*And when I stood in that field and all was dark, I did not sense any malicious intent. No ill will. It was only the nature of things.*

*This feeling is in you as it is in me. You just need to listen to it. You think it all some secret though. A finding. A discovery of a distant land you are long on the path to. Yet it reveals itself as a remembering. You have already arrived. It will just ask you to surrender so it can open up to you.*

*I know what this feeling is. I cannot tell you though. I can show you.*

*I do not question it. I cannot. It makes no sense. All I can do is follow it. It is my nature. It is your nature.*

*It is the nature of things.*

# Chapter One

## Common Hours

Horses are my heaven. In their presence I feel something that brings my world together. What I hope they feel from me is friendship. I hope they feel I'm someone who loves them very much.

I walk out to see Rocky in the fields where he lives. The walk beneath the fresh daybreak sky rouses the life within me. Matea jogs ahead. The Siberian husky's fur flows from chocolate to golden brown and then on to white paws. She was an orphan puppy when I first met her, abandoned at a shelter after having been attacked by an adult dog. Surgery left her face a little crooked, but the dog inside was unchanged. *Beauty is not a look, it's a feeling*, she says. And nowhere is the dog's beauty seen more than in her eyes. One brown and one blue. A sharp, reflective, unbroken blue. Like the sea illuminated by some great underwater sun.

We walk up over a hill and there's the herd perfectly scattered around the field. Each horse attends to its grazing and I hear the chewing of the closest one. The sound rivals any music. The five horses—two bays, a buckskin, a black-and-white paint, and a palomino—belong here as if grown from the landscape. Part of the land as much as the grass and rocks and trees.

All continue eating except the palomino. His head is up and he's looking at me. His golden-yellow coat glistens in the sun and his platinum-white mane floats in the breeze. The four white socks and the white blaze running from forehead to nose are tailored perfectly to the horse. As he watches me approach I feel his eyes as if he were right in front of me. He is farthest away but my connection to him transcends any distance between. There are times I'm at the barn and I feel something, almost hear something, and I turn and he's looking at me from across the field.

He takes a few steps toward me as I come up to him.

"Hey, Rocky," I say softly.

His presence settles me. His softness inside finds the softness in me. I reach up and rest my hand on his withers. "How's the herd? You guys happy?"

He looks away, casually taking in the surroundings. His jaw loosens and he turns his head sideways to yawn. I chuckle. Like he's laughing too he gently nudges my shoulder, then lets out a deep breath and relaxes his head next to mine. I lightly rub his nose, that perfect texture of fuzz having a feel only nature and its billion-year-old ways could create.

I am most commonly called a horse trainer. I travel to homes and barns and listen to horses and people and help them as best I can. That's how I see my role. People are perplexed when they learn I didn't touch a horse until the age of twenty-six. But when I'm with a horse I'm at home. Soon the people, just like the horses, don't care where I come from.

The people that call me are looking for something. It starts in so many different ways. I'm looking for something too. I see the work as an equal set-up between the person, the horse, and myself. It's an opportunity for all of us to come together to learn and grow. But deep down there's something else going on when we work with a horse, and it's present in every moment. The feeling that what we're really doing is learning about life. ✓

Henry David Thoreau wrote *If one advances confidently in the direction of his dreams, and endeavors to live the life which he has imagined, he will meet with a success unexpected in common hours.* Life isn't about getting somewhere or obtaining something or finishing something. It's about knowing what we are drawn to and confidently advancing toward it each day. ✓ Success will then come to us, many times, in ways we don't expect, through all the days. Those common hours.

There was a time in my life when I was lost, and I searched across the land to find what was out there. In the end, it brought me around to looking inside myself. The journey was simply the means of opening me up to it. I found a connection to horses, and beyond that, a connection to myself. And now I am confidently advancing toward both of those connections as best I can.

Endeavoring to live the life I imagine.

I walk into the riding arena at the Common Ground Fair. Around one hundred people watch as I close the gate and turn to face Rocky where he stands in the middle of the arena. I walk to him, he walks to me. We stand together for a moment and then I place my forehead against his. "Let's show them our hearts," I whisper.

My hand glides over the palomino's neck and settles at his withers. His eyes softly blink and he lowers his head and looks to the ground. He paws the dirt, searching for the feeling. He settles somewhere within, a moment of opening, and he lies down. I kneel beside him, softly running my fingers through his mane, saying to him, "Thank you, Rocky."

I slide my leg over until I'm sitting on his back. I lean forward and rub his neck with both hands, burying my nose in his mane and soaking up the greatness of that immortal smell. I lean back and settle myself. His ear turns back to me, and then his eye. He's ready. "Up we go, together."

Rocky stands up with me aboard. Once upright, he brings his head around to nuzzle my boot. "I'm here," I say.

We ride with no saddle or bridle, just human and horse. I begin moving my pelvic bone in the rhythm of riding a horse at the walk. Rock feels it and some voice inside him says *we are walking* and he walks. He gets in-sync with me, all in the great search to feel another and move forward with them.

"It's in all of us," I say to the people watching. "We all can do this. [Every human and every horse can tap into this ability to connect with one another.] It starts with finding a feel for where you are yourself. Then you feel for the horse. If you can't find either right off, that's okay. The horse will help you. Being in their presence is all you need to do. From there you just gotta start slowly, softly, and have an open heart to wherever it takes you."

In my thoughts I see Rocky and me trotting. My hips start to move as if we are. Rock feels the change and picks up into a trot. We turn, do figure-eights, pick up speed into a strong trot and then slow back to a jog, all with the same intent, all with a balance between, all with the same softness within. I breathe out and slow my motion and we come to a stop. His powerful body relaxes but is still at the ready.

"You can see in any horse, any animal, any human," I say. "You can see what is in their mind. There is power in what we

see and feel, and power in what it projects. The way to a smooth
canter is to see and feel a smooth canter, not to hope against a
hard and rough canter."

I feel for the canter. I feel Rocky feeling for me. Both of us
are searching, working our way inward for the feel. Our movements would just be the result of that [We're looking for what's
in our thoughts, our feelings, our spirits.] When we find that—
feeling good together in that great good place of the soul—it
will color our canter with brilliance.

Rocky and I together feel the canter. I move my body as if
we're about to pick it up. He pushes from his hindquarters, his
core strength ignites, his back rises strong, he arches through
his neck, and he flows up and forward into the most beautiful
of canter strides. [When a horse seeks the rider's guidance and
freely chooses to do what they ask, it will naturally use all its
strength and balance in its movement.]

We canter a few circles and I breathe deeply and slow the
motion of my seat. He eases back and we move into a trot. I
slow myself more and we walk. I cease all forward energy and
Rocky stops. I slide my left leg to his shoulder and upon feeling
it he looks to the ground, searching for another feel. I wait. He
walks here and there, spins, finds a spot that suits him and lies
down. I step off his back and kneel beside him. I lean forward,
close to his neck. His scent settles me in ways only it can.

I stand. "For thousands of years horses have been at the
mercy of humans," I say to the audience. "We needed them
for our survival. So we dominated them and forced them to do
what we wanted, and they've given their lives. But there are
new ways of inspiring horses to work with us."

Rocky stands up.

I whistle and move sideways, and Rocky shifts an ear my
way. His eyes follow, and he turns and squares up toward me,

readying himself for what I may ask. "That's the important beginning right there—getting his attention. If we get a horses's full attention, and then use our energy through our body language to show them what we'd like, horses are very open to following our guidance, all without any pressure pointed at them in any way. We need to start there—getting a feel for our own energy and body language as well as the horse's) And through this we'll develop a feel for how much the horse is *with* us."

Rock's attention stays with me as I talk to those watching. I bring up my energy and ask him to follow me, drawing him toward me. I walk around the arena and he follows. We run, stop, back up, move sideways, and then stop in the middle. I raise my hands to cradle the sides of his face and he lowers his head into my chest. His eyes soften and I give him a good scratch in his ears.

"And the eyes. How they feel about what you are doing is always in their eyes. The old ways of horsemanship were just about how to get the horse's body to do what we wanted for travel, for pulling, for farming, for wars. We dominated horses mentally and physically solely for our benefit So horses gave us their bodies, all when their minds could be checked out, gone, defeated.

"But if a horse's mind is *with* us, if the horse is choosing to be with us out of its own free will, and being with us feels good to them... its body and all its strength are with us every single time. The whole horse.

"The most common way a horse is trained, though, is with some sort of pressure we apply to them that is released when they do what we want. What's essentially happening is the horse is moving away from a feeling it doesn't like. A swing of a rope, a kick of a human's heels, a pull on a metal bit—a feeling *we* are providing, no matter how small or large. And when a horse is moving away from a discomfort we are providing, it's really moving away from *us*.

"There are two motivations out there really. Moving away from something that feels bad, and moving toward something that feels good. And choosing to do something that feels good runs so much deeper than moving away from something bad. There's a place we can get to, where the horse has freedom to make its own choices. A place where they choose to follow our guidance. Where they get as much out of the relationship as we do. A place of mutual respect that feels good to *both* of us. There comes a point where what the horse is feeling while it is doing what we ask becomes more important than what we are asking."

I look to Rocky and close my eyes. I breathe in deeply and slowly exhale. I open my eyes and feel my heart beat slow. My eyes softly blink. I feel my body relax.

I continue to talk. "And after all the tries and mistakes and successes, you and the horse develop a feel between you. Something that guides both of you together. You'll start to hear a guiding voice deep inside you, clear as day. You won't know where it comes from but you'll trust it. And you don't *learn* this voice. No. It's always been there. You *remember* it."

Outside the arena stands a woman. We do not know each other yet. I don't see her standing there, and won't meet her until a few months later. She watches Rocky and me, feeling she somehow knows us, though.

It's said that souls plan their meeting long before they meet in this world. But if I had been told of what was coming, would I still have chosen it? If I knew of the fantastic love and the ferocious fear... the bounding joy and the searing pain...

No matter, those thoughts.

There's no turning away from the voice once you hear it.

# Chapter Two

# Wild

*I am wild.*

*I feel it every day, this nature the world is built upon. It is there to fill me up and keep me coming from that great good place. To be free to live as I am meant to with the company that feel right. They help me to feel good and I help them to feel good.*

*Within this freedom there are laws though. Rules to the wildness. And these laws treat all equally. Like gravity. Gravity treats all the same. If we step off a cliff, we fall. Some fall harder than others, but all feel that pull downward. It is always there. A law.*

*The more these laws are understood, the less battles there are against what does not change. Like with a physical body. The brain guides and the muscles create motion while the bones give structure. There are rules to bodies, such as the laws of nutrition and the laws of motion. If you work with these rules, you move strongly forward. Disregard them, and you break against them.*

*Then there are the other laws.*

*Laws that make life interesting. These are the laws that govern choices made and actions taken. What is unique to you, and never the same in another. Unlike the laws of the physical world, these internal laws cannot be seen or touched. You can feel their weight but you cannot weigh their weight. A choice made from love creates a different result than one made from fear. There are no rules, no laws, no governing force written in stone to dictate these choices. But there are indeed rules as to what happens from those choices.*

*Matters of the soul are given true freedom to sink and to fly, to soar and die and be reborn again. Pure infinite magic that is never the same twice. What is consistent though are the feelings associated with sinking and flying. Follow love, and life gives back in great ways. If you do not, life gives lessons. And through it all, the journey feels endless and eternal in scope. Always happening, always seeing.*

*And wild.*

*And when you are wild with another, when you both share a feeling, when you run together through the fields...*

*You see that being wild is really just being in love with life.*

—ᗰ—

A friend calls me. "There's a magazine you gotta check out," she says. "You and Rocky are in it."

It's a piece about the fair we were at. The images in the article catch my attention. There's no *trying* in how they were shot, as if taken on a whim. And the photos don't show us doing anything really. They are of moments, times I can't even remember. It's as if the photographer was in the arena with us, invited. I see Rocky and myself on that day, but I also see all our time before that day. I see our first meeting when he was a fuzzy little foal with no trust in humans and I was a young excited kid learning from horses how to trust in myself.

Whoever took these photos wasn't taking pictures of just a person and a horse. They were capturing what was inside us.

The article is about the Common Ground Fair. It talks about its history, its mission, and how it got started. It features the vendors, the artists, the organically grown food, the educational seminars, the focus on family. It then goes on to talk about the livestock area and the demonstration Rocky and I did:

> The man and the horse look like they are not leader and follower but instead friends. The horse is so much larger than the man yet that fact seems to disappear. He uses no equipment with the horse at all, and what they do together seems so safe. There's an intimacy that flows between them. They perform well together but sometimes get out of sync. The man talks about it, speaking of how that helps them learn and grow, and how it helps bring them closer. He says their work together is not about getting anything right, but instead the feeling they share while trying. I forget I'm watching a person and a horse. All I see are two souls that have traveled together and are deeply connected for it.

The article was written by a woman named Calla Viaje. I search for her on the internet. She is a photo-journalist, and lives an hour from me.

I look up from my computer and see a bird fly past the window. I can't make out what kind it is. It looks like a dove. It flies up and over the trees, then floats along in a current unseen but trusted by wings made perfect for the cause.

—m—

When I was young I could feel something ahead. Something we all have ahead. A destiny, a path we're on. That pull forth to do this or that. How much of this path is born into us versus how much is created along the way I never really thought about. I just felt it. There was always a feel for that great road ahead and what it would bring, and *who* it would bring.

It was there in so many stories, this search for someone to love and be loved by. The whole world seemed to think it was one of the main focuses of living. So I set out in search of it in my everyday life, feeling an unsettledness I was sure would go away once I found it. But a question would come now and then... did this search come from a feeling that I had love to give? Or was I searching for someone to provide the love I thought I lacked?

I write to Calla, thanking her for the photos she took and the words she wrote. After exchanging a few messages we decide to meet. On the walk to the coffee shop I suddenly get nervous. I open the door. She's sitting at a table facing me, settled and relaxed as if alone in the crowded room. Our eyes meet and neither of us looks away. I stand in the doorway, she sits in the middle of the cafe. The place is bustling with other people but they're not there right now. There's a two second span when we see each other for the first time. A pristine glimpse of all inside that is eternally and unapologetically trying to free itself to the surface. I stand in the doorway. She sits there by herself. And I feel that everything this world is here for is suddenly here.

We both smile. She rises to greet me. I walk to the table. By the time I get to her I'm completely at ease. We shake hands.

"It's nice to meet you, Calla."

"It's nice to meet you as well," she says.

We sit across from each other. Her posture is relaxed and confident. Long and wavy chestnut-brown hair evenly frames the delicate features of her face. It flows over her shoulders before falling down her back. Her green eyes give while asking nothing in return. I feel an immediate safety to be who I am.

"I'm happy you could meet with me," I begin. "What you wrote about Rocky and me was beautiful."

"It was amazing watching the two of you. It went right to my heart," she says freely.

I smile. "Your photos did the same for me."

She smiles. "Thank you."

"You do that type of work for a lot of magazines?"

"Yes, I have to." She chuckles. "To make it work as a photographer and writer I have to work for a lot of publications."

"Have you been doing it long?"

"My whole life. Getting paid for it though, about five years." She smiles and keeps easy eye contact. "And you work with people and their horses for a living, right?"

"Yes, one-on-one and I also do clinics where I work with groups of people."

"Does Rocky go with you?"

"Oh no. He just comes with me to the demonstrations like the one you saw."

"You two have quite a bond."

I think about the moments in the photos she took. "There's something there between us that's pretty tight. It's as much from the hard times as the good," I say.

When I speak she listens. Her whole body is poised to soak up every word. She listens, feels, thinks, then responds with her words and posture and gestures bound as one.

"How did you guys come to know each other?" she asks.

"He was young, having a hard time. And I was young, having a hard time," I say with a smile. "I happened to be in a place where I could help him. And he's been helping me ever since."

"The hard times seem to take us further."

"Agreed. There's something to that for sure."

"The union of pain and a higher understanding." She smiles, lightly at first, looking me in the eye, and then the smile bursts from her face. Love for life that can't be contained.

We tell each other our stories. The tales that tell what brings us to who we think we are. The stories we tell ourselves. The stories we choose to believe are us. We freely converse of love and fear and letting go and forgiveness and each thing effortlessly leads to the next.

"I believe," she starts, "that all of life is one. That we all come from the same source, what most of us call God. And our journey here on earth is one of growing through the challenges we face. Where we deepen our understanding and capacity for love. All while on the road of learning about ourselves and what life is."

"Wow, you got that squared away pretty nicely."

She laughs and puts her face in her hands. "I didn't say it was that easy to live it, though."

I laugh, then speak seriously. "I agree. I totally agree. It's a journey that's all about some sort of… growth that happens along the way. And as we learn, our experience of life definitely changes with it."

"It's the hard times, though, right? Those are the times that take us the furthest, but we're so scared of them, so scared of being hurt."

"That's the hope of anything that's alive, a desire to avoid pain. It's built into us. I mean, I look back at the things that've hurt me the most in life, times when I've been hurt, times when I was the cause of hurt in another... and I would've done anything to be out of it."

"But now, looking back, how do you feel?" she asks.

"I wouldn't change a thing."

She looks right at me. "Now what about the current things that are hurting you. Can you have the same respect for them, right now, as you do the past times? Can you appreciate them right now while you're going through them?"

I look at her. "Well... that's the hard part of it all, isn't it? These times, the current things that are hard in our lives... it's hard to be thankful for them," I say.

I talk with a nakedness I've not experienced. I listen with all of my being and inhabit her words and understand them as if my own. Like I have nothing to lose I say what I feel. I don't think, I just speak. Honesty is so easy. And during this whole time there's one thing gloriously missing. I am more enthralled with another human being than I have ever been in my life, yet my mind is not taking me into any thoughts of romance.

Maybe I don't have time. With the moment so beautiful, and with me so wholeheartedly surrendering to it, maybe the future and all its possible outcomes that usually spin around in my monkey mind simply doesn't have space to exist. The moment wants for nothing and for once in my life I'm not getting in the way.

Afternoon weaves into evening. Hours pass. It's dark outside and I look to see what time it is.

"Wow," I say.

"What is it?" she asks.

"We've been here for almost five hours."

Her eyes go wide. "What? Really?"

We leave and walk side by side on the way to our cars. The talk opens to silliness and laughter, a decompressing. Something shifts. I become self-aware in a way I wasn't the past five hours.

"Well, my car is this way," she says. "It was great talking with you. Do you hug?"

"Yes," I say.

We hug. A simple, free from everything embrace.

———m———

Her eyes look at me and leave no room for anything but truth.

The mustang runs around me in terrified circles. Her wildness screams for any opening of escape. *Don't think, just run.* She runs circle after circle with the primal fear of death in her eyes and a wake of dirt exploding into the air behind her. She is Cheyenne, a thirteen-year-old mustang mare, born in the wild and captured when she was two.

Captured, but never tamed.

A movement too hesitant or too fast on my part and the bay-colored horse will be gone in a flurry of runaway. Her self-preservation instinct is on overdrive. She has spent the last eleven years of her life successfully fending off domestication by humans. That's eleven years of running and fighting and winning.

She can barely be touched. She trusts nothing in her world except her own sense of escape. People have spent many hours just sitting with her, trying to help her open up. But the moment she senses a person's intent is on her she's gone in an eruption of snorting and hooves and dust. Saving herself by imprisoning herself into the same view of the world over and over again.

Because she can't be handled she can't go outside with other horses. She can't be haltered or led, so if she were to get loose there would be no sure way of getting her back. So Cheyenne spends her days turned out in an indoor arena and a small paddock just outside her stall.

I keep telling her she doesn't have to trust me, I just want her to know she's safe and for her to give me a chance. My intention is simple: I want to help her open to the possibilities. She keeps saying *no, I am not safe. Not as long as any human is near me.*

"You are safe, Cheyenne, with me and with the folks here that are looking after you. They just want to take care of you and for you to feel comfortable being haltered and led."

After spending time just sitting with her, I approach from her left, breathing easy, eyes lowered, blinking, and my shoulders relaxed. I smile. Horses know the difference between a smiling human and one that isn't. Never have my energy, presence, thoughts, and body language been tested so. Everything in me has to be aligned. A stray movement from my pinky finger and she'll be gone.

She wants me on her left eye, as most horses do. When fearful, worried, or just having to think, most horses prefer humans on their left eye in the beginning. Leading horses on their left? That was their idea, long ago, not ours.

I advance, and retreat back. I search for an opening. I look for curiosity. I wait for a moment of understanding, a seed of confidence. Eventually I am three feet from her. I take a step forward, then a step back. She stays protected. Her bow is pulled back and an arrow is ready to fly.

I stop.

We stand for a moment. Cheyenne's left eye locks on me. What that must feel like, to stare at another being and hope it doesn't kill you. It's not surprising many military veterans feel a bond with horses.

I breathe out and extend my hand toward her and...

In an explosion of survival she's gone and sprinting circles around me. I can't do anything right now. If I try I will only stir her up more. So I walk to the middle of the pen, kneel down, and wait.

She runs from that ingrained instinct to flee until she comes to an abrupt stop and stares at me from that left eye.

I tried. That's what was off in me. I was *trying* to move softly. I was *trying* to look non-threatening. I was *trying* not to be hesitant. And trying is different than *being*. Cheyenne sees trying as *faking* and faking means you're hiding something.

It isn't a horse training thing, it's a life thing. It's about naturally being calm, soft, and confident and just letting that do its thing. Just *being* it. Letting it permeate through my movement, communicating to all around me that I'm a friend. I *am* calm and I *am* soft and I *am* confident. The horse feels your whole life and reacts to what you have spent all your days becoming. I just need to relax and be what I am in this moment.

I take a deep breath and let go of all wants.

I remember back to when I was young and loved just being around any animal I could find. I didn't try to be gentle, I just was. It was in me. I loved all animals and my sole intent was just to be with them. I didn't *want* anything from them.

After a few minutes I get the closest I have ever gotten to Cheyenne.

We stand facing each other. Our breathing is like words telling our stories. Without choice my hand slowly starts to rise. She wavers and leans back but something holds those fleet hooves in place. She stands, some unseen power anchors her there with all its might. She's feeling the same urge every human and animal feels sometime in their soul—hold steady and find out what's there. Wildness knowing it's connected to all other wildness.

Forget inches, this is a game of centimeters. If I break and think about what I'm doing for a moment, she'll break and be gone. I have to let my hand follow the feel. Extending, pausing, retreating, extending again, movements all governed by some inherent sense coming through. Not wanting anything, but just being.

Cheyenne stretches her neck toward me. I gently let my hand move to meet her nose. Her whiskers brush my hand and she sharply pulls back. I do not. My relaxed pose reassures her. She holds, stands. I am not hesitant. I have no tension on my insides. I'm not waiting for her to explode. I am waiting for her to relax.

She hesitantly stretches her head back to me, and with that I gently rub her nose. I softly lower my hand and stand there. She watches me and waits. I turn and walk back to the middle of the pen and sit down.

She looks at me with curiosity, processing the idea that when she runs from her fears they have a habit of following her; when she faces them they have a habit of going away.

"Rounding you guys up, taking you from your natural lands, separating family groups, and then locking you up in steel pens," I say to the mustang. "That must be so traumatic. Those pens must feel like imprisonment to you."

Cheyenne stands and barely blinks from that left eye as she watches me speak. She hesitantly turns her head so that both eyes equally look at me. Then, as if afraid of being caught for doing it, she quickly pulls her head back so only her left eye is on me again.

"I know there are many factors involved in what's going on out there in the wild horse situation. But you don't know that. You see it all pretty simply. You were just living your days as they came. Living in nature, by your nature, and trusting in the balance of nature. You can't get more wild than that."

Cheyenne has lived free in the wide open land and now I speak freely, forgetting who I am and what I came here to do. Again she looks at me from both eyes.

"And if you guys are strong in your herd numbers, then good. People can adopt more mustangs and slow the over-breeding of horses that we're doing, which is the root cause of all the horse slaughter in the world. You guys make great partners, you connect so deeply, I think because you've lived in the wild and your spirit runs deep. You're naturally confident with a strong work ethic. You've had to work for your survival. Some of you are pretty easy to work with right off too. And people are learning to love *being* with horses, not just riding them, and not just judging a horse by what it can do for them."

The wild one stands. Is she dumbfounded at what this human is blabbering about? Can she understand me? Can she read my body language as I talk? Can she see the pictures in my mind? My energy?

"It's not about some place we hope to get to, you and I. It's about just being in the moment, together, here and now. And that will take care of tomorrow."

She stands there not taking her eyes off me. I feel her wanting to come forward. Without wanting it I see it. Her body isn't moving but her whole being leans forward.

Then she blinks her eyes, blinks them again, lowers her head, and takes a strong step forward into the great land of *what can be*.

# Chapter Three

## Days in the Fields

*You have a guide that is always there.*

*What you feel shows you the way. It comes from the great nature born within. You can choose to follow it or not. There is freedom. Moments pass and come again, and feelings pass and come again, until they are listened to.*

*Feelings do not lie. They speak of what lies ahead. Often what guides you is not how you feel during an experience, but knowing how you will feel as a result of that experience. You feel when something is going to fit and when it is not, even before you do it. And the only way to see this, is to let go and be taken for the ride.*

*You are here to feel and grow, and to help all around you to do the same. How you come to know this is by connecting to yourself and all the world around you through relationships. Some stay for a short while, while others go the distance. There are no rules as to how long they endure. But the lessons learned never leave. They do not know time. The connections made never leave as well. They are always with you whether you see them or not.*

*You will know when a choice is right. Your feelings will be your guide. Hone them. Know them. Believe them.*

*Trust them.*

—m—

A lone path carves its way through the woods. Matea jogs ahead. Calla and I walk side by side. We decided to meet again.

"Sometimes I see a photo," I say, "then I go to the place where it was taken and it's not nearly the same."

"The moment has passed," Calla replies. "A photo is its own thing, complete in itself. I've never thought it was solely meant to represent what's pictured. So much goes into taking a photo—the angle, the light, the balance, the timing, and the moment—a great collaboration. And then there's the deepest element involved, the feeling the person has when taking the picture. It's a meeting between the beauty being photographed and the feeling of the photographer."

"Two things reaching out, looking for the middle between."

"Exactly."

"There's an author, Tom McGuane, who once said that when a horse and a human move together as one, they seem to become a third greater thing."

"That really speaks to me," she says.

On the drive here to meet Calla I felt many things. Excitement to see her. Passionate about what we would discuss. Joyous in how we would connect. Relaxed from wanting nothing from her. Free from expectations. In love with how I felt just sharing space with her. Inspired by how our time together would leave me feeling. Intrigued by the mystery of what she was. Amazed at how all these thoughts would vanish once I saw her.

It's as if thinking can't keep up. Thoughts come before and after, but during my time with Calla my mind shuts off. The constant babble in my head, that steady stream of back-and-forth chatter simply disappears.

A bald eagle flies over us.

"Look at that," she says, smiling. "I could watch that all day."

"Do you usually carry your camera with you?"

"No. Sometimes I just want to let life be and not get in the way of it. The camera can separate you. I think it would be like when you're alone with a horse versus when you're doing a demonstration. Do you sometimes feel different?"

"Yeah, I get what you're saying," I say. "I used to be pretty insecure when I was doing a demo with Rocky. I would worry about us looking good. A lot of my self-worth was tied up in how people viewed us."

"How is it now?"

"Well, I realized if I just kept myself in touch with the feeling of connection with him, that whatever happened from that, whether success or failure, was really the same."

She smiles and looks down at the path, stepping over roots that have breeched the ground and extend across the trail like petrified tentacles frozen in their grip upon the earth.

A few weeks after our walk I invite Calla to where Rocky lives. She arrives and I greet her. We head out into the open fields where the winds sweep across the land. Her brown hair floats and flies and settles around her with the softest of touches. Soon we see the horses ahead and sit down in the grass to watch them. Amazing messages are exchanged at such quiet times. It's no mistake land like this is long respected. No mistake a horse sees it as home.

"I love it here," she says.

"You feel it?"

"I can feel it and I can see it. How they move. How they stand. How they go about their eating. When they swish a tail for a fly."

"I believe they live with the feel of a wild horse herd," I say. "They graze as a wild horse would, moving over the landscape. They come and go as they please, for water and shelter when they want it. They make choices. They get to live."

Calla soaks up the sight. "They have their own lives to live," she says.

"Not much different than humans."

"Yeah. Makes me think we don't need all we think we need to be happy."

"I think it's not about them catching up to our ways. It's about us slowing down and getting back to their ways," I say.

"Back to the peace that comes from just living."

My eyes settle on her. She's dressed in a long red skirt with a white linen shirt hanging off her shoulders. A tight black tank top underneath. Her brown hair falls down over her shoulders and her green eyes sparkle with love for the day. Her truth inside easily shows outside. Spirit offered into form. Like the wind through the leaves on the trees, the beautiful invisible is honored into something seen.

She smiles and points up ahead. "Here he comes."

Rocky walks toward us with interest. He slows as he gets closer and extends his head to Calla. He touches his nose to her face. She smiles and lets this happen without worry.

"Hello, Rocky," she says.

Rocky blinks. Then blinks again, and again. He breathes out strongly and classic horse spittle sprays over Calla.

She laughs. "Awww, thanks, Rocky!"

I smile and just watch. The horsemanship side of me wants to be alert and watch how close his feet are to her feet. But all is okay. I don't need to get in the way of this moment. Something stronger holds it together.

"His presence is so soft," says Calla.

"That's one of the coolest things about horses. They don't see size. There's nothing in them that thinks big means anything."

Her hand finds its way to his ear. Or maybe it's Rocky finding a way to put his ear in her hand. She gently scratches and Rocky helps by lowering his head and leaning into it. Both human and horse with blissful eyes.

Later in the evening we build a fire. Horses graze and the sun goes down.

"It seems like... something's changing," I say. "Humans have spent so long trying to master the world. We've been tirelessly focused on conquering nature, the land, the animals. Trying to bend it all to our will, and using up a lot of it along the way. Everything in me feels like it's now time to slow down and take care of it all. It's time to give back. After all the planet has done for us, it's now time for us to take care of it."

"I believe we're all feeling that," she replies. "If you ask anyone I think they would say they want to see the land and animals taken care of. It's just a question of whether we can let go of the things that get in the way of that. Can we be serious about the new ways of being we need to turn to."

I put another small log on the fire and stare into the flames. "Humans have grown through civilization and created amazing things," I say. "It feels like it's now time to grow inside ourselves and create amazing things there."

The horses move around the field, drawn to do this or that by some force that guides us all. Matea lies on the crest of a small hill and watches the land. Her contentment towers over any need.

I watch the horses. "Just... love. They're in love," I say. "We can't always see it clearly because we've separated ourselves a lot from it, but a horse or any animal, they're just in a constant state of love for life, their existence, and all the good and bad of it. Actually, I'm not even sure they see anything as bad. They just live. They don't get in their own way. They don't think about what's happened to them. They live and learn from what happens and then let it go, moving on and letting the future come. And they don't know if they're to live one year or thirty, they don't sit and worry about it. They just live. And they don't leave anything left on the table. They spend their days. They live from their instinct and wherever it takes them. And in this way they live in some sort of constant gratitude as well."

A long pause. Calla's gaze fills me. I've never felt someone listen like this. Never felt so understood, so safe knowing I would be heard.

"We see things in them, and we are reminded of the same things in ourselves," she says. "We recognize we're like them. And they us. They help us to remember where we come from and what we're here for."

We stare into the fire. Whenever we stop talking there's a silence like none I've ever felt. A fitting kind of quiet. It feels safe not saying anything. The silence speaks in ways of its own. *Being in your presence is enough*, it says. Just like the way horses stand with each other and share space, side by side in silence, saying more than words.

The last cries of the sun cut through the pines as it drops from sight. The sky deepens into the cobalt color of cold ocean. The conversation eases into talking about past relationships.

"How long were you together?" I ask.

"Three years," she answers with her eyes still in the flames. "We met through work. I was immediately attracted to his open-hearted embrace of life, the excitement he had for it, like he could do anything. It proved hard to be in a relationship together, though. Just learning how to move together, I don't think we ever found our way in that."

"Not the easiest of things."

"It was like we just couldn't find our rhythm. We both deeply wanted to be in a steady and stable relationship with each other. But it always seemed like when one of us was wanting to stay close to home, the other was wanting to be out traveling the world. The timing was off."

"For all of the three years?"

"Oh, there were good times." A trace of a smile shows itself in the light flickering over her face. "There was him playing the piano for me on Sunday mornings. Us helping baby sea turtles make it to the ocean on Padre Island. The random kidnapping of each other and then driving without knowing where we were going…"

She is deeply affected. I listen, feeling no need to offer anything but that.

"I got frustrated with the lack of stability, though, just as he did," she continues. "Soon we were seeing only the hardness of it all when we looked into each other's eyes. We both thought we were giving our best. Resentment built up. Neither could let it go long enough to just breathe."

The fire illuminates her face in the dark. I see her eyes staring through the flames into some portal to another world that will live on forever. She turns to me and says, "We just didn't speak each other's language."

I look into her surrendered green eyes and watch the left corner of her mouth curl up into a slight half smile. An honoring to the time from ago.

"Try as I might," I say, "I can never even remotely think or believe or ponder that my past relationships were mistakes in any way. The good times and bad. The love, the heartbreak… I've never felt it could have been someway else."

"So you think it's destiny, whether it works out or not?"

"I don't know. It all seems… needed. And if I had done something differently, then I wouldn't have met Rocky or Matea when I did. So I gotta honor the past and what happened and how it happened."

"Do you regret how anything ended, though?"

I think about the times when I walked away or watched my loved one walk away. I think about the times when I wished I had done something differently. The times I didn't do enough. The things I didn't know how to do. The things I chose not to do because I was too mad or too scared.

"Edward Abbey said something once," I say. "That in stories, readers should experience what he called the inevitable surprise. They should be surprised by what happens in the story, experiencing it in the moment as if they had no idea it was coming, but in the very next instant realize it *had* to happen that way. Well, I think that's how living goes. We don't always know what the future is bringing, but when something happens, we eventually realize it had to be that way. It's a balance. The fate within our freedom. Like when I was sitting with a girlfriend once, we were out in a field, and I knew she was about to tell me something that was going to hurt. And when she told me, instead of getting swallowed up by the pain of it, something in me… shifted. Something let go and opened up and what rushed in was a love like I'd never felt. I wished her well, hoped the best for her, supported her, and wanted to see her in love, even if it was with another."

Calla smiles. "Do you know what that feeling was?"

"I believe it was my first true experience of giving unconditional love. And I couldn't have gotten there without all that
happened before it. It all made perfect sense, how everything
lined up."

She smiles deeper. "The inevitable surprise," she says.

We both sit and let the silence speak.

"Do you think love ever goes away?" I ask her.

"No. Because I think it's always there to begin with."

"Are you ready, Kim?"

She smiles and looks away. "I guess so."

Kim is in her mid-forties, and she begins leading Faith, her
twelve-year-old paint mare. Faith is new to Kim, a horse she
found on the internet offered for sale at some archaic auction
in some faraway place. Nobody wanted this horse. Faith was
going to be sold to the highest bidder, someone who would
most likely sell her for slaughter. A kill-buyer, as they're called.

Kim walks. Faith follows. The horse is nervous and so is
the human. Their nerves bounce off each other. It's easy to
see that Faith has never trusted a human before. She's scared
of them, all of them, and what they might do to her. Kim is
scared as well. She feels like she's in over her head with this,
she tells me.

None of this mattered when Kim first saw Faith, corralled
in some small pen with her life in doubt. Kim couldn't get
away from the idea of helping her. So she did what she could
do that day. She bought her. What would happen after that, she
didn't know.

Kim walks and Faith follows but they are not connected.
The horse's attention is on too many things. On the tree-line

nearby, on what Kim might do, on what I'm doing. Kim recognizes this and knows getting the horse's attention is the beginning. Only then will Kim be able to talk to her, only then will
Faith be able to hear.

"I feel like I'm on one end of the lead rope and she's way
over there on the other," Kim says. "Disconnected."

"What would happen if you took the halter off right
now?" I ask.

"She'd leave."

"What does that tell you?"

"That it's the halter that's keeping her here, getting her to
do this. That if we ever ride, it would be the bit and the reins
she would be going with, not me. Her body is with me, but not
her mind. She's not here."

"Yes. And when she's under stress, whether from you or
something else, her body will try to go where her mind has
been the whole time. To the gate, the barn, the other horses.
Wherever she thinks is the safest place."

"And that's not with me," Kim says.

"Not yet," I say.

Kim stands there holding one end of the lead line and
looking at Faith on the other end. They may as well be a mile
apart. Kim stands there and feels for a way ahead, searching for
a vision that will take her and Faith forward, an idea that comes
up through her that she'll instantly know is the way. She has
always called herself a beginner. Her family recently bought
a farm and Faith was their fourth horse. They purchased Faith
just to save her, with no expectations of what the horse could
do for them. But it mattered if Faith could trust Kim and follow
her lead. And so here we are.

Kim slowly starts nodding. "Okay. I gotta believe in myself.
I gotta be mindful, present. Start slowly with one simple thing

and get a feel for it, something that's easy for both of us. One thing that'll give us a feeling of what *right* feels like. A feeling for what being with each other feels like with her attention and her *try*. Once we can find that, and know what it feels like and how to get there, then we'll have a beginning."

"Sounds good. Watch her body language, see the movements, but also see beneath them to what she's thinking, and beyond that, what she's feeling. It's not just getting her to move how you ask, it's what she's thinking while doing it that will get you to the connection."

Kim begins leading. She moves with intention. She has a vision of what she wants to have happen. She asks for Faith to follow. The horse tightens its neck and widens its eyes and waits for the tug on the lead rope.

"Remember, don't just pull on the lead rope or swing the rope at her to get her to move," I say. "Help her to choose to come with you. Find a way to her mind. The body will come with it, every time."

"Faith," Kim says toward the horse. Still nothing. "Faith, with me," and this time Kim follows her words with a strong accentuation of her body language and a clap of her hands. "I'm here, please look at me, Faith. I know the way for us."

This stands out to the horse. Faith turns an ear toward Kim, then turns and puts both eyes on her, all while softly blinking. After a moment she walks a few steps in Kim's direction and stops. They stand like this for a while. Kim then walks to the left and Faith follows. Kim then turns and walks to the right and Faith follows, all while taking steps closer to Kim. She has the horse's attention and the horse is naturally beginning to seek the feel of her guidance.

The power of choice versus the power of pressure.

Kim uses her energy and body language to keep Faith's attention and then draws her to come with her, leading Faith by inspiring her to follow. With confident intent Kim walks left and Faith follows. Kim then turns right and the horse follows. Kim asks and draws and leads. When she starts to lose the horse's attention she uses her energy to get it back — picking up the pace; changing direction; saying Faith's name; scuffing her feet to get the horse to think about her — and when Faith comes back, Kim immediately gives her something to do. And because Faith is choosing to follow, she moves as light as a feather with no contact on the lead rope or halter needed.

They continue walking together, Kim leading Faith like the horse is her shadow. To keep Faith's attention, Kim keeps things interesting, turning and stopping and backing, along with changing speed, tip-toeing and jogging. All with slack in the lead line. The difference between leading a mind and leading a body.

"Do you feel how your energy rising or lowering is not threatening to her?" I ask.

"It's just talking to her," says Kim without looking at me. "Talking *with* her, not *at* her."

"You got her attention and then gave her mind something simple to follow that felt good. Horses and humans love moving together, in-sync, when there is no pressure from the other involved."

"It feels wonderful."

"Yeah," I say. "Who doesn't like the feeling of having a guide? Someone we can look to? You're being that for her. Getting her attention, helping her to follow your feel, and letting it feel good to both of you."

Kim stops for a moment and stands with Faith.

"And see what you were called to do there?" I say.

"What?" asks Kim.

"What your gut told you. It said to stop and stand for a moment and let things soak. These in-between moments when you take a break and stand together, that's when the feeling of connection sets in. You just *be* there together and let the great feelings of what happened settle in to you. And how would you be able to know how strong she's with you now?"

Kim takes off Faith's halter, and the horse stands there with no change to eye or movement.

"There it is, the great beginning change," I say. "Her choice to be there with you, something you never told her to do or made her do. She simply wants to be there, and the body goes where the mind is. And when you work with her next, there's the chance she'll start off following you simply because she wants to find the feeling again."

"She'll look for it."

"She'll look for you."

Kim, Faith and I stand in silence for a while. Kim then asks for Faith's attention, picks up a feel with the horse through body language, and they begin walking together again. I watch intently. The feeling grows inside Kim. Her energy... her eyes... her movement... they all work as one, unified, and talk to Faith. Kim feels the life of the horse with her. She feels a mind. She feels Faith.

There's an alive feeling between them. Faith thinks, Kim doesn't. Kim is moving with a feel and letting it take over. She moves into position to yield the horse's hindquarters and Faith understands. Kim's energy speaks to her, and the horse yields her hindquarters as long as Kim holds that position. Kim then gets into position for the forequarters to move, Faith recognizes this, and does the movement as long as Kim is asking.

Kim takes a deep breath, and I see in her eyes that she's cen-
tered around an inner vision of all she wishes to have happen
here. She's moving and acting and preparing as if the horse is
going to be with her in all ways. They move into doing circle
work. As they work together, Kim and Faith are in-sync, then
out of sync, then in-sync again. Sometimes on, sometimes off.
Constantly swimming around in the feel for each other.

It's like following the motion of a glove that's mysteri-
ously floating in the air, animated by some unseen power, and
you're trying to somehow get your hand into it. Your hand
gently follows the glove's motion, trying to synchronize with
it. It follows the motion of the dancing glove and bit by bit
it's able to softly slide into the glove, still moving with it, letting the motion be. Soon the hand fits into the glove all the
way, wearing it, and the hand eases into the lead of the motion.
The glove takes on the hand's guidance and direction and they
move as one.

Soon, just like a hand in a glove, the human and horse move
as one with no perceptible difference between them. Kim's
feel, in its inner archaic language, connects to Faith's, with
no boundaries between animal and human. Both bonded in
the great universal relation. Faith follows, not behind but *with*,
immersed into the feeling of moving with another.

They approach the mounting block. Kim asks Faith to
stand beside it. The horse centers herself with an eye and an
ear on Kim, and Kim climbs the steps and then lies over the
horse's back. The horse steadies herself, helping Kim to get on.
Kim gets her leg over and sits there. They are where they are
supposed to be. The natural progression without expecting it.
Being there because it's simply the next thing.

*Will you carry me* is in Kim's eyes.

Some place inside Faith says *yes*. And she stands there, carrying Kim, with no halter or bridle. Nothing holding her there other than her own choice.

Never wrong or right, just in touch with what is.

Within us is the energy to create our path ahead. It's the taming of this energy we're in search of. Once we discover a feel for it, we also discover we can create our future in a way that doesn't take away from anyone or anything, but instead inspires all.

# Chapter Four

# The Feather Bed

*The biggest fears are actually the biggest opportunities.*

*I have seen falls. I have seen blood. I have seen gashes and swelled joints and broken bones and I have seen death along with them. I have also seen the one thing that is worse.*

*Avoiding any chance of pain.*

*In the quest for safety so much is lost. It is no fun falling down, but it is a disaster to be kept from the possibility. Life comes with death, and acceptance of this leads to happiness. Life actually comes with many deaths during it. Beginnings and endings. Much changes as you experience these lives and deaths. But always there is that one constant that does not change.*

*You are safe.*

*You can take that chance. You can take that leap. You might get hurt but if you know your heart and follow it, whether with a small step or a giant one, you cannot fail. Whether successful or not, what awaits is the same. The mistake is thinking that surviving the leap is everything. Because just by taking the leap do you get all you came for. What you pay in courage is paid back in love.*

*Giant leaps cannot be taken all the time. True love and courage can sometimes mean taking a step back. True daring can be choosing another path. One way feels right and the other does not, and you take your best shot at coming from your heart. Whatever then happens is never wrong. Because nature is never wrong. Just like you are never wrong. Mistakes are really just results showing the truth of things. They show you where you are, and if you listen, they also show you what you need to do.*

*You are born into the journey of figuring things out as you go until the day you die. Searching for your heart and tying your leaps of faith to it. With that comes injury. Sometimes you see the injury, sometimes you just feel it. Cuts show trying. Scars show healing. Loss shows love.*

*Whether you take that leap or not, the same thing is always there to catch you. Jump and you will be caught, land and you will be caught, fall and you will be caught. Do not jump and you are caught. So go forth and live by the heart. Sit in silence until love speaks and then advance toward that feel. Forward is freedom. Leave it all spent on the path. Feel life. Feel all of life. Feel all the fear in the world and take the tiniest steps forward knowing you need fear as much as love.*

*Know that fear is love.*

A dirt driveway leads into the farm. It's usually busy with people and all they do with horses but it's eerily abandoned this evening. The hazy glow of floodlights is my only welcome. I park and turn to the back seat.

"Just me this time, Tay Dog."

Matea looks at me with that one blue eye and one brown, ready for whatever adventure I've driven us to. She knows what my words mean, though, and lies back down with a sigh.

Dusk is settling in and bringing a chill with it. The even sound of my footsteps comforts me, my canvas jacket warms me, and my frosted breath in the electric night air inspires me. I walk to the horse's stall and open the door and go in and stand with him. A young thoroughbred, dappled dark gray, and tall and strong and fast. I wait for the feel between us to settle. My breathing, his breathing. The place he's at, the place I have to remember. My hand settles on his forehead. I feel all of him, all of a horse's life. I run my hand from behind his eye, down his neck, along his back, down his hind end and leg, and all the way to his rear hoof, tracing the bladder meridian. This has a calming effect, influencing the sympathetic and para-sympathetic nervous systems, which helps relax the fight/flight response. After I do this on both sides he turns to me and touches his nose to my chest and his gentle eyes show a quietness behind them.

His name is Max. I lead him out of the stall, and see how he feels about putting his saddle on. I take my time and he allows me. We walk to the riding arena and start our work together on the ground. I wish to guide him and for him to seek my guidance. I begin leading. I focus on bringing him into a mutual rhythm with me. I move with confident intent, unified within. After having him yield his hindquarters and forequarters, I ask him to go out to the end of the line and circle me. His ear and eye are on me, his thoughts with me. His head and neck are raised tightly but slowly relax and lower. I breathe and his breathing comes with mine. We move together, sanding away any miscommunications, and when we find the soft moments we pause and share space, letting it soak. When he feels steady and with me, I put the riding halter on him.

I gather the reins and place my foot in the stirrup, breathe, and look to Max's eye. A horse tells a story in this moment. In the eyes is always an instant truth. And in his I see the frustration of his past.

Max had been sold from a racer. Most horses are judged by how well they perform for us and like endless thousands before him he was sold when he didn't measure up to somebody's expectations. A modern day slavery. Humans suffer from the tragic belief that animals are lesser. The woman who bought him was committed, though, and wanted to do right by him. But his young energy would constantly boil over, making it hard to work with him sometimes. Combine that with this boarding barn and how it's stifling to him. It isn't horsey here. It has only the convenience of the human in mind. Small, dark stalls with the horses confined to them most of the day. No real land to live on, be alive on. No horses to be in a herd with, to be a horse with. And now the horse can't help it. He has no filter from his insides to outsides. Because of his past and now his present living situation, the actions of the horse, those visible colors of the soul, are frustrated and angry as he chews the wood in his stall, bolts away from those who try to lead him, and bucks off riders when they try to ride him.

A horse's natural mindset is to give, but through some discomfort in the body, some ill-fitting saddle, some lack of getting to be a horse, something confusing or scaring or rushing or cornering... and then they say *enough*. The bite, the spook, the kick, the buck, the rear, the bolt. Our brace becomes their brace. It's reflected back at us, exposed, presented to us in the highlighted form of the horse's behavior.

Max and I begin riding, feeling the rhythm of the walk, my center and his center finding a mutual center. In the sway of his back and the sway of my seat our bodies connect. My reins and legs have a soft feel to his head and sides, like I'm holding his hand gently and confidently. My eyes see our way ahead. His stride is long and relaxed, his neck level with the ground. The horse and rider at the walk is pure beauty. The great beginning.

It's late and electricity is in the air. Sounds from outside the arena expose the tension in the horse. We ride in figure-eights. This simple course keeps his body bending and his breathing loose, and the frequent change of direction keeps our thinking on each other.

Whatever is to happen here is of my own creation. The horse was standing in his stall when I came to him. What I get will be from what I give. Every great canter or ferocious buck will be brought from my choices and what I put forth into the world. The horse simply a messenger.

He puffs up, his energy building. His head is high now, his neck and jaw tight, and his eyes aren't blinking. I think of dismounting and spending more time with him on the ground. Always an option at any time if I become uncomfortable.

"I'm with you, Max," I say as we move into serpentines. "Let me guide you. I can show you a way where we both feel good. A place that helps us, takes us to new places. We can get there, together."

The words I use are important. Voicing my thoughts out loud creates the pictures in my mind, and I believe horses see the pictures in our minds. They feel them in the effect they have on our energy, on our breathing, and on our body language. The effect they have on our feel. And I just plain believe they see the pictures in our minds.

I need to get doing something to keep his mind with me, to loosen us up more. "Let's move together," I say. "Smooth and balanced, with me in the lead. It's good for me and it's also good for you, to follow my lead. So here we go, a soft walk flowing into a soft trot." He picks up into a pretty trot with a good feel. After a while he relaxes a bit through his body and breathes more slowly and deeply.

But there are noises in the woods still. He's concentrating so hard it's born tension along with it. I relax more, bend him in simple ways, filling in for him. My eyes stay focused in the arena and I turn left, then right, then left again. Then a fig-ure-eight. All in an attempt to keep his mind with me. Instead of waiting to see what he's going to do I take the lead and create something good. Action leads, reaction follows.

He comes back to me.

"Thank you, Max."

But the evening noises escalate. They won't let go. It seems it has to happen. Maybe in order for us to get over it. Sometimes we have to break to find out what's on the other side of it.

He twists and spins with a squeal. His head drops and his hind legs kick into the air and his body arches into a good-size buck. I relax, deepen my seat by leaning back, and move with him. I slide my left hand up on the rein and bring it wide away from my body. He turns and once his neck softens later-ally I add my left leg to yield his hindquarters. The energy in his body lowers and he comes back to me. The one-rein-slow-down. Meeting anger with peace is truly the way to peace. But we must also be prepared for what may be thrown at us when another is off balance.

"We're okay... you can relax. Your owner knows. She's looking for a new barn, something with bigger fields and more time outside, a herd you can live in. She's thinking of what she can do to help you."

He has been trying hard for his new owner. The buck is a left-over habit. A residual. A reaction from older times. Self-preservation, what led to most attacks on others.

Fear, in some way or another.

I redirect him and we keep working, getting to the good stuff and letting the bad fade away, as it's destined to do. He calms, lowers his head, and softly blinks his eyes. He licks and chews and then slowly breathes out, expelling old air from his nose in the great way horses do. That great waterfall of relaxation.

And we canter.

I feel Max searching. He's searching for the feel between us, looking for me and who I am this evening, seeing what's really here right now, and letting go of the past getting in the way of the present. Taking a leap of faith that all will be okay.

He's surrendering. But not to me.

To the moment.

I let the feeling soak in for a while and then we walk, letting it all cool. We end with a feeling we'd like to begin with the next time we meet. I step down out of the saddle. Old leather creaks and he turns to me and I look into his eyes and there it is. That great realization that changes your whole life with horses and how you forever see them or any animal. The understanding that Max cares just as much about his life as I do mine.

I extend my hand to his forehead and his eyes soften. My breath and his breath mix in the frosty air and for a moment they become one, our breathing merging into one white swirly stream.

The magical made visible.

—m—

*Are you available to meet with me today?* I ask Calla in a text.
*Yes*, she answers.
*Where would you like to meet?*
*There's a park down the road from my house.*

On the drive to meet Calla I think about the challenging horses I've worked with. How so many times I wondered how it would come together. How so many times it found its way. All the horses I thought I would never be able to ride but then came the time when it felt right to ask them to carry me. So many times when I felt it was right for someone I was working with to try something with their horse. So many times when I rode Rocky free in a field or on trail or at the beach.

There were also those times when things didn't go as planned, though.

Since first seeing Calla sitting there in that coffee shop I have been completely in awe of the connection I feel with her. And now on this day my intention is to tell her my heart is feeling something more. Why today? I can't say. Like horses it doesn't know time, only the right time. All things have their moment, and it was time to tell her my heart felt more than just friendship for her.

I park the car and take one last look at my hair. All good. I get out and open the rear door and Matea jumps out. We enter through a gate and see Calla sitting in front of an old tree at the edge of a forest. Matea runs to her. The dog does her squeaky-bark hello and then softly rears into the air to give Calla a quick lick on the face. A dog hello, given every meeting as if nothing is more important. Dogs are teachers of what matters.

"Hi, Tay Dog," Calla says.

Calla stands and we hug, holding it for a moment. The conversation has already begun. A feeling of safety comes over me, no matter what this day holds.

"Hi," I say.

"Hey there," she says.

"It's beautiful here."

"I love it. City forests hold a lot of stories."

We go for a walk and the small talk hangs in front of what sits in my mind. I'm not nervous, though. Walking with Calla I cannot help but feel the security in her presence I've always felt. I feel no fear, just the adrenaline of living by my heart. My only intention is to put words to it all.

When our talk eases into a natural silence I feel the opportunity. We sit cross-legged across from one another in a grove of trees. Matea lies beside Calla. The people I see walking nearby give me confidence. The day is surrounding us, supporting this stage. The way the wind blows through the leaves seems to gently ask me to speak.

"Calla..."

"Yes."

"There's something I wish to tell you."

"Yes..."

"When we met, as we've talked about, I felt an immediate connection," I say. "Spending time with you, talking with you, getting to know you... it's been amazing."

She sits with a feel of leaning forward into me. She wears her hair up as if choosing no guard. Her green eyes blink less and less as if wanting to stay open. Her breathing slows as if feeling my words.

"And through it all nothing has got in the way of it," I say, smiling. "No feelings of *is it this, is it that?* I've felt nothing but wondrous connection and, more than anything, I've been so thankful for your friendship."

"Thank you. I feel the same," she says.

"You've inspired me in so many ways, and I'm so thankful for that, for you, for meeting you, and for the time we've shared. And I want you to know... nothing changes that. What I'm needing to say is about me and my heart, and how you feel is honored no matter what."

The words come and I trust them. "And what these last months have led to for me... are feelings that go beyond friendship," I say.

Her eyes do not change. She holds them fast to me. The feeling of her leaning into me doesn't waver. Her openness expands.

"I feel the same way," she says as she places her hand on mine. "During the last months I've felt a connection to you that's very strong and it felt so comfortable to just let it be. Everything in my heart came without trying. Sitting here with you, I have feelings that go beyond the friendship we've shared. I can say that now too."

In the space of a moment a new freedom exists. Life changes just from new thoughts alone. The whole life I've lived up to this moment feels now like such a beautiful journey.

Later when we walk from the forest and are about to part ways, I finally get nervous. Should we just hug, or should I kiss her? Thinking abounds and suddenly I'm that kid on stage not knowing his lines in Mr. Hilton's eighth-grade drama class.

"Um, alright... so I guess I'll see you in a few days or so?" I say, caving in on myself.

"That would be great."

I hesitate. I decide to just hug her. I'm in doubt so I retreat. A tip-toe of faith instead of the leap I lived by earlier. We hug and smile and say goodbye and she walks one way and I the other. Something left undone. My moment of stepping back in fear stands out among an afternoon of stepping forward from love. There's an ending that doesn't fit.

But I'm alive. That means at any moment I can choose something different and be the thing I once wasn't.

I turn around and walk back to her. "We forgot something," I say.

She turns around and her eyes and smile unite in innocence. We embrace and kiss. I try to lead the way but I can't seem to find the feel. She seems to be trying to lead the way as well. The kiss ends up being like two dancers who haven't danced before but think they have.

She starts to giggle.

I laugh. "And there's my awkwardness finally making an appearance," I say.

"Don't worry. It goes well with my goofiness."

We pause to just look at the other and smile. Still letting it find its own way.

Matea and I go to see Rocky. The palomino horse watches us approach from the other end of the field. His eyes ask *so how did it go?* Maybe I'm reading into it, this inquiry. If I feel good, I see him feel good, though, that's for sure. So I guess how it went matters to him.

"Well, I did it, and it was beautiful," I answer as I walk up to him.

He turns his left shoulder to me, wanting a scratch. I bend my knees and lean into it and scratch away.

"Yeah, and you'd be proud of me. I was confident and relaxed and spoke from my heart the whole way, and all with no fear it seemed like."

I stand with him not in celebration but in comfort. I'm living, doing my best, that's all that matters. I'm opening my heart, more every day, laying it out there and setting it free. What comes along with that is simply just living. I stand with Rocky and Matea, united in that we three lived this day doing as we were drawn to. In love with life and all that comes with it.

Terence McKenna said "nature loves courage... this is the trick... this is the shamanic dance in the waterfall. This is how magic is done. By hurling yourself into the abyss and discovering it's a feather bed."

The wind picks up and silently blows through Rocky's mane the same way the wind blew through the leaves of the trees at the park and I feel a security in whatever happens from here on out.

# Chapter Five

# Little Things

*You feel for magic.*

*The most common place it is found is in relationships. The ties to loved ones, to the land, to experiences, and to the great mystery that is life. It is through relationships that the glow shines most.*

*Like all of life, a relationship has a pulse. It lives and breathes like a wild animal. It can be content and it can be enraged. It feeds off whatever is offered to it by those who bore it into existence. It assumes a life of its own. It requires you to constantly feel for the balance between yourself and another. You sense the balance exists somewhere, so you search and feel and work until you find it. And each time you find the balance, you learn the feel of it so you may return. You find the magic that reveals that your heart lives in another.*

*Day or night, awake or in dream, you look for the clues that guide you closer to yourself and others. The little things of each day always serve to bring you closer in some way. You discover what opens you to friendship and love. Even when the hard things appear to be pushing you further away, they are not. All experiences help in some way to show that love is always present. Until you are able to feel that, there will be hardships that will come to try and show you what you do not see.*

*Sometimes the little things go unnoticed. You try so hard and work so hard and take everything so seriously, thinking that everyday life is just monotonous content between the big things you seek. And somewhere the priority becomes making life comfortable and without challenge. You fall into a cycle of the same days over and over. Avoiding hardship equals a pulling back from life. Eventually you look out over the horizon and feel something big and beautiful is out there, but not within you.*

*In the little things of each day are opportunities to experience life in a new way. There may be challenges, but the whole process can be loved. This cycle of growth is constantly going on within. You are endlessly feeling for yourself and others. If you slow down you will see the gifts of greatness in the little things. There is always beauty. You just have to remember.*

*When you slow down, you not only see the little things, you also see the big things before they happen. Big things are just the result of little things. You can see the signs and understand them and know what is coming, then act if you wish to create new little things that will lead to new big things.*

*But if you only see the big things then the secret will stay a secret.*

*That there is no difference between little things and big things.*

We lie naked in each other's arms. Her wild green eyes are stirred yet content. She smiles and closes them, brings her body close to mine, and softly laughs so lightly the sound can only be for my ears. She opens her eyes and they look into me and they love me, they say, and I feel the love my heart always felt for her, even before I met her. I can see and feel the love, and for the first time in my life I *am* the love. The deep love I have for Calla allows me to see the deep love she has for me. My love for her shows me the truth of all things. This love that needs and asks for nothing. All I need to do is get out of its way. Her look, her smell, her touch, her laugh… it's all I need and with her I somehow magically become who I've always wanted to be. She's unlocked my life.

"I've always felt I was one step behind the man I knew I could be. With you, Calla… I feel I *am* him. Life has caught up with my dream of it."

She smiles and her whole body moves in unison in some beaming, grateful way. She curls up next to me and nuzzles my neck like the most innocent wild thing. "You know what?" she gently asks.

"What?"

"You're magic."

I smile.

"You're perfect," she says. "Today and all the days before. You're enough and always have been. I'm so thankful, for all of who you are."

She smiles and cozies up to me like she can't get close enough. Her hand runs through my hair. What comes from her touch is electric and capable of dropping me to my knees or lifting me into the heavens.

"Worth it," I say.

"What is?" she asks.

"All the days that have brought me here. I've never felt so trusting in life."

"All your days, the good ones, the hard ones… the happy and sad ones… they all came from your heart. And your heart is love. It is. It's true. I see you. I always see you, in all you do. I saw you that day I first saw you, at the event with Rocky. I saw what was between you. And I saw what was in you. I saw *you*."

"Do you see me right now?"

"I do." She closes her eyes and nestles her head into my shoulder and hugs me. "And I love you, so much."

"I love you, Calla. With all of me."

I've never been so honest with another; never has another been so honest with me. Our communication is open and we listen with reverence. There is such care in our relationship, so much honor in this love, and a trusted sense of safety in where it will take us.

We go on adventures. We make dinner together and watch movies late into the night. We talk. We speak our truth with trust there's nothing we can't say to the other. We express our love and give it freely. Talk of the future comes freely as well. As our relationship moves beyond one year, we speak of the world we would love to live in, together, in coming years.

Support for one another is a priority. In thoughts, words, actions, and by just holding space for the other, listening to them. Hearing their experience. We are there for each other and when someone helps you through your fears you bond to them in ways not of this world alone.

"I love your smell," she says so many times.

"Really?"

She buries her nose in my armpit and inhales. "Oh my God, yes."

All the stuff I think is the weird stuff, the weaknesses, the points I'm sure will push her away, all the particulars about me I fear letting her or anyone in on… the more I let them fly, the more she loves me. The perfect guy I'd tried so hard to be my whole life does nothing for her compared to my weaknesses.

My hardships bring her closer. She wants the real. She wants the me I am when I'm alone. The more vulnerable I am, the more she tightens to me. The more I surrender to who I am, the more connected she feels.

This relationship wants only truth. All relationships are endlessly vying to get there. But I don't know if I would've survived this any other time. What I feel for Calla, this all of my world love, I don't know if I could have handled it earlier in my life.

But I'm ready. So I let the truth fly and leap into the unknown. And again and again she catches me.

—〰—

I lie in a field on an August day and the grass is a miracle. I marvel at the silky feel of each blade. I wonder what makes it grow. Not the sun or the temperature, but what causes all things to grow. What is the invisible power underneath all that is. What flows through the universe and moves everything along a path of life and death. This blade of grass I stare at is on that path. Its own destiny within the great flow. The last thing I want to do is get in the way of that. I leave it be.

Matea lies nearby. I can feel how content the dog is. She lifts her head, her nose picking up an invisible scent passing on invisible currents and telling its secrets to her. She looks over to me and when I look into her eyes I feel an ocean of connection. The Tay Dog knows all of me as sure as she knows the smells in the air.

The only sound behind the chirping of the birds is Rocky's munching. He could be a wild horse right now, grazing in the fields and casually watching the life around him. The way his eyes blink, so soft around the edges, sends a wave of joy through me.

Lying in the grass here and just watching everything feels like something I could do forever. Has some dormant love been awakened within me? Because now my eyes see everything in a different light. I see love and connection in everything. Someone laughing is like love bursting forth, someone crying is like love feeling for itself. Wherever I am I want to give and help and inspire. I want to give back to the world that's giving so much to me.

I sit up and Matea and Rocky look to me. "Ready to get moving, guys?" I say.

I get up on Rocky bareback and bridle-less, a free horse, and we ride around a small grove of trees to see the herd grazing. Tay Dog jogs through the band of horses with her tail up and waving like a proud flag. I feel Rock's steadiness under me in his relaxed top-line, in his secure steps, and in his blinking eyes. When I breathe and look to the left and my body shifts, he turns. My hands at the base of his neck help guide him. We move straight for a while with my body evenly following the sway of his back and the push from his hind legs and the forward steps of his shoulders. When a horse is truly with you, you don't feel their size, only their feel. And right now Rocky is as light as a feather.

The more I feel the love within, the less I feel I am without. I look out over the herd of horses and I feel so much love for them in just what they are. Beautiful in their horse existence. I sit atop Rocky and we visit with them, talk with them. I pat their heads from atop his back. One of the horses, Whiskey, walks along with us for a while. There's a wondrous curiosity in his eyes about what we are doing and an interest to be a part of it.

As we move through the herd I realize it's not about what we're doing. It's what we are feeling that interests him.

We ride back to the barn. Matea is already there lying in the shade. I slide off Rocky's back and smell the faint scent of horse sweat in the breeze. A hot day bringing out the life in us all. The wind dances through his mane and speaks of a good day.

"It's okay," she says. "You can tell me."

We sit in our living room. We have been living together for a while now. She's facing me, but I'm staring at the floor while she looks into my eyes and waits. The love is strong still. But we also have our hard times. This is one of them.

"I know," I say in a quiet voice, my body clenching. "This isn't about you, you've done nothing wrong. It's about me and how I see things."

"It's not just that, I play a part in this as well." She leans her head lower to insert her face between me and the floor until we're making eye contact. "I do it too. You've seen me when I get in my head."

I look into those green eyes. It's so easy to love her. "When you made reference," I begin slowly, "to that guy you were working with, and how much fun you had, I got... I wouldn't call it jealous, but..."

"Scared. You got scared."

"Yeah."

"I know. I do too," she says with gentleness. "With all the women you work with in your job, and you walking out that door everyday in your boots and hat..." She laughs the fear off, shaking her head at it all.

"Calla, when I leave this house I go through my day as if you're walking right beside me. In all my words, in all my actions, I do it all as if you're standing right there with me."

"I know," she says. "That's how I feel too."

"We have trust in one another, we both know that. But I guess that doesn't mean we're free from fears, though."

"No, seems they'll be there sometimes," she says with a smile.

We laugh and something is expelled. We hug and hold each other. I feel the heat of her body.

"I love you," I say.

"I love you," she says.

We have worries and wonders, scares and fears. We see how vulnerable and exposed we are. We each go quiet at times when something resembles a time from the past that tore into us. We see how our pasts have formed us into protective responses the moment a situation resembles something that hurt us. We know it's not the other person hurting us, but our own minds seeing the old situations that did. Moments from long ago that are not the moments of now. It allows us to see the little things, the beginning moments where these haggard thoughts come from.

We see how the fears coming up within us are actually opportunities. Hidden pains have been exposed and brought to the surface, and we have an opportunity to clearly see them and how they work. We see the little things that bring them alive. In that moment we can let go of the fear, the doubt, the insecurity, the anger and all the stories we tell ourselves about what makes us do what we do. We have the chance to move beyond what is holding us back from a deeper experience of love.

We always end up closer for it. We never regret. The hard times open us and show us something deeper. Whether it's Calla or me who falls out of balance, the other is there in mind and body and spirit until a coming together. It usually starts with little things. One night she comes home late without calling. One day I get up without acknowledging her. But the dedication to our love always leads us to something greater. We're both calling forth all the heart and soul we have to make this relationship work. We're all in. So we do the work. And we connect deeper and deeper.

We openly talk of how our coming together feels like it's for the whole way.

"You're my one," she says.

"I love you, for all of the way," I say.

The horse and dog love Calla. They feel what's in her presence. Her touch and how she talks to them. It's in her, a love for all things, especially the furry ones.

She loves Matea as if the dog is her own. Calla respects her as an equal, easy to say but hard to hold up to in our dealings with the animals. But she does it. To see her and Matea get excited when they greet one another is like watching two old friends, one with a smile and the other with a wagging tail. To watch them both together in their own relationship is amazing.

I sit back and watch as Calla stands with Rocky and talks with him. I know both of them so well and love them so much and to see them together warms me in all ways. She doesn't try to do anything with Rocky. She lets the conversation between them develop on equal terms. His gentle lips massage her head as she scratches his shoulder. *This is it*, I say to myself as I watch them. This is what I'll remember. This is what I'll take with me through the days. Through this world and the next, this is what stays.

It's what drew me to horses in the first place. Not to ride them or see what they could do for me, but just to be with them. To stand with them and scratch their shoulder while they nuzzle me with their nose. In Calla and Rocky I see an innocence that the young horseman in me remembers.

Seeing this all together is the most beautiful thing. Matea leads, pausing to look back and check in with her pack, followed by Calla and Rocky walking side by side. I walk behind so I can see it all.

Every now and then I catch Rocky looking to me. I make eye contact with him and I hear a voice, and whether I ever know it at the time or not, what's in that voice is always true. What's behind those eyes always finds a way to guide me to what's right there in front of me.

I'm watching a family walk together.

# Chapter Six

# Season of the Bolt

*The mind tells you that you can hurt only so much.*

*You are born knowing you will die. The fear of losing your life dictates so much of your thought. You think about saving yourself the moment you feel threatened. You may be standing there doing everything as normal but in your mind you are getting ready to run. All it then takes is something sudden or shocking and you bolt.*

*I know what this feels like. This self-preservation instinct born into every living thing is a gift, for it keeps us alive. Your body is the vehicle with which you interact with the world so you want to keep it alive as long as possible. The mind is where you experience life, so it is just as important to keep that alive. This instinctual need to protect them is a great gift that is honed to perfection every day of life. There is also a mission underlying our existence: to live and grow and pass on everything to the next generation. And the longer we stay alive the more we pass on.*

*What also comes with this protection instinct are braces that get created over time through experience. Innocent enough, they are responses created by that self-preservation instinct* that get triggered the moment a situation resembles something that hurt in the past. Even if there is no real threat, even if it is all just made up in the mind, it does not matter. The mind sees something and feels the pain of the past which then shades the sight of the present. Thinking gets blocked, the mind has already made its decision. You become braced, and to those around you, your brace makes no sense. If pressed, you defend. If pushed, you shut down. If cornered, you fight. If in fear for your life, you bolt.

It can be a threat to the body or it can be a threat to the mind. When something gets hard in the head it can cause a bolt just as easy as being chased by a bear. There are times when getting away is the right thing to do, but there are also times when a challenge needs to be faced. When challenge is avoided, the prize is getting to stay safe. Safe, but the same. Wanted when running from that bear sure enough, but regretted when you realize the bear was made up in your mind. When you run from this understanding of yourself, you block the living that could help you get over your troubles. You run from the discovery of new worlds. You save yourself only to imprison yourself.

There are times to walk away and there are times to step forth. But you cannot do it until you can do it. Because if there is rushing, if there is pushing, if there is forcing... there will be a bolt. A mind not ready and forced to face its fears learns only how to run away better.

When you bolt, the reality of present moments do not matter anymore, for you are living in the past to keep yourself alive. Bit by the bear once, and now seeing big teeth on everything.

The mind sacrifices possibility for safety. You have chosen to stay alive at the expense of living.

The sounds of morning. That moment of being in a dream and awake at the same time. My eyes flutter open and I breathe and I feel her hair against my skin. Her head nestled into my chest. Her sleep-ladened arm across my stomach. Her satin-smooth leg entwined with mine. All of her body's warmth passing into me. I hear her breathe. I feel her breathe. I close my eyes and immerse myself into her. The separation between our bodies hazy. The outlines fading. Where one ends and the other begins unimportant. Our hearts are in one body.

Matea gets up from her dog bed and walks beside our bed. I hear her sit down with purpose to let me know she's there. It's customary that she's allowed up with us in the morning.

"Hop up, Tay Dog," I say.

She springs up. The dog walks around in her tight instinctual circles until her ancestors and what they learned and passed on tells her she has found the right place to lie down. She takes a deep breath and settles in. Dog happiness.

I listen as the two of them breathe. Matea's breathing deepens and soon she is dreaming. Her body contracts to and fro; a muffled bark calling from the other world. Barking, chasing, living... all while warm and safe in this bed with us.

Calla moves slightly. She's half awake. Under her breath she utters a soft and small sound of contentment and she draws herself closer to me. Slight movements in her legs or hands and I feel them as if tidal waves pouring over my body.

Mornings like this are the point of living. As I lie in this bed, I feel an invisible force field around us, and no words or actions could ever penetrate it. With love comes a seeing behind the curtain that everything is love. Even the bad things. The constant chatter in my mind—the worry and wonder and *what if*— is gone and replaced with some sort of knowing that all's okay.

The relationship is not without challenge, though. We fall into times of not feeling safe, brought about by some perceived slight, some lack of attention, not enough of something or too much of another thing. The mutual balance we aim for is elusive. It dances on currents we can't predict, on air we can't see. One believes one thing and the other believes something different, with each sure of their thoughts, ready to stand their ground, steadfast in their conviction of what they are feeling. We become defensive and look out for ourselves, not wanting to let go of how we see things and give in to the other's point of view. Not wanting to let go of the only thing in the world that has ever truly comforted us—our belief that we know something.

"Why do you always do this?" we say to the other.

"Why do you always put it on me?" the other always says back.

What was the issue this time? Was it me bringing up a past relationship and her then shutting down? Or was it me shutting down after she brought up her ex-boyfriend? Did I get insecure when she broke plans? Or did she pull back when she thought I wasn't around enough?

After each clash we have a hard time remembering where it began. The exact cause is as elusive as remembering the exact things said. The words seem to fly out and fly away. All is forgotten each time except the feeling we're left with afterward. People will squeeze each other forever until the end of time. The only thing that ever changes is what's inside waiting to come out.

"Why don't you ever listen to me?" she says.

"I listen. I hear everything you say. It just gets tiring to constantly feel like I'm doing something wrong," I say.

"Because nothing ever changes."

"You don't change either."

"You blame me for all the things your ex did that hurt you," she says.

"Like you don't do the same?" I say.

"Well you blame everything on me and—"

"Well you blame me for—"

Matea comes out of nowhere to hurriedly press herself against my legs to get my attention. *Look at me! Look at me!* In her eyes is a desperate eagerness to help in the only way she knows. *I'm here! I'm here!* Her tail wags in anxious sweeps across the floor as she does all she can to throw me off the present course. *Do something other than this!*

But I'm not able to see her right now. "It's like any time I do something that makes you feel uncomfortable, anything at all, you want me to change so it's more comfortable for you," I say.

"You get defensive any time I bring up what I need for help in this relationship."

"Because you don't take any responsibility for our hard times."

"I'm honest when I mess up."

"I am too."

"I want this relationship to work, but it's hard when I'm the only one that's trying," she says.

"How can you say that?" I say.

"This just... this isn't working. I can't keep doing this."

"What are you saying? We should end this?"

"Is that what you want?"

"That's the last thing I want."

"It's the last thing I want too."

She starts to cry.

I look away.

She sits down on the floor.

I stand there.

Her crying goes full on into sobs, head bobbing.

No words come. I can do nothing but watch. My heart knows all I need to do is go to her and hold her and all of this will go away.

I lean back against the wall, my body deflates, and I hollow. I slowly slide down until I sit on the floor, my knees pressed against my chest. I hear her crying. I cannot look.

I finally choose. I crawl to her and hug her. She wraps her arms around me and I feel all of her love. Her tears flatten against my cheek and spread across my face.

"Are you okay?" I ask.

"I don't know. Are you?" Her eyes are so vulnerable. She could be carried away by the slightest breeze.

"I am." I want to be okay enough for the both of us. "I'm sorry." Never have I wanted my words believed more.

"I'm sorry too," she answers. "I know you give everything in your heart, and I love you with all of mine. Do you know that?"

"I do. My heart feels for yours all day. Do you feel that?"

"I do."

She reaches for my hand and takes it in hers. The way her body fits into mine, two pieces of a whole rejoicing when brought together. We rest our foreheads against each other's and close our eyes. I see the stars of our galaxy. The cosmic colors of our souls. Our great heaven and the odyssey we travel within it.

I look into her eyes. "Why do we go through this?" I ask.

"I think we're caught in... some sort of dynamic, a cycle that keeps bringing us back to this." A lone tear streams down her face. It speaks of wild and fragile love. "We have things we need to work on," she says.

"I know."

We go on. There is talk of new days, new choices, new ways. We connect, letting our love lead us, but we also get lost, letting our fears derail us. The times begin to rise and fall like two kids on a teeter-totter, one laughing, one crying. Moments holding each other, the perfect kisses to cheeks in the middle of the night. Moments in fear, the cold confrontations questioning commitment. We believe we have the dedication to get us through. We listen to the other, hear each other. We forgive each other's mis-steps. We're giving this love our all. If it should break, it won't be from lack of love nor dedication to the work needed for it. No. If it falls it will be because of one thing.

That it's not meant to be.

The sun bellows down upon me. The arena footing feels hot through my boots. I look into the surrounding trees and I see a light breeze dancing in the leaves. The green of the trees flutters and floats. It speaks of moments coming. Times when you later realize you felt what was going to happen.

Oakley and her owner, Brianne, walk through a crowd of spectators and enter the arena. They are to be the sixth horse and human pair I work with today. It's the second day of a two day clinic, and the other five people are done for the day. Sweat has dried on my face, concreting all of the day's dirt within it. It's that time of day in a clinic when I can't drink enough water, a combination of being in the sun and talking so much. I'm tired, but ready. I am where I want to be.

Oakley is a young quarter horse and percheron cross just learning about riding. Brianne is doing the work herself. She is confident but doesn't have a lot of experience with younger horses. They have ridden bareback and under saddle, and both horse and human are comfy at walk and trot. Brianne lets me know that when they tried the canter Oakley got going too fast and she fell off. She has been reluctant to try again.

I feel I know the horse. The feeling in the groundwork is there. Attention, a try, and confidence. It seems we're on the same path with our intentions together. She's a bay-colored horse, stocky and strong, and her young years and energy let her move with spirit and sureness.

I feel good, talking with those watching as I step into the stirrup and up onto the horse. My legs settle to Oakley's sides, my hands settle into the reins. I breathe and my body finds its home on the horse. With all that is conveyed through this, all of who I feel like to her on this day, we begin.

When we are around a horse it can't help but feel who we are, or rather *how* we are. How we feel to them begins the day we are born. How we live, how we are raised. It continues as we are taught by those looking over us. The influence of our friends plays a big part. Our choices become ingrained in us, and where they take us becomes a part of us as well. Of course we can change at any moment, no label or past has to stick unless we let it. We can cast away our personal histories at any moment we choose. But how we live walks with us. It brings us to where we sit on our horses, and it's with me now as I hold the reins in my hands.

The trotting goes well. I feel for the thoughts in Oakley's mind and they're with me. I change rhythm, direction, soften the bend in her neck, and yield her hindquarters to a walk. As we move I see the attention we're both paying to each other, I see the try we're both putting in, and I feel the confidence between us. It doesn't mean perfection, though. Life is life. The experience of it includes all things.

I visualize us cantering. But I'm thinking about other things too. I can't not, it seems. All the stuff that's worrying me in life. Fearful thoughts slide in through any crack they can find in my focus. I read what the horse has to say. Her inside ear is turned back to me, she's level-headed, and her eye is blinking. My seat eases into the circular sensation of cantering. My outside leg softly comes on to the side of the horse and massages in an inward-circular fashion that fits with her movement. My inside leg gently opens but keeps a small feel at the girth for support. My outside rein maintains a soft feel while my inside rein opens, guiding her thought and bend. A whole world in that moment of never-ending little things with Oakley and me the creators. And we canter.

She bolts. Her mind lets go and some volatile lying-in-wait thought ignites and she explodes into a gallop. She's a rocket in the form of a horse. A machine of nature using all its raw power to flee.

I am supposed to stay calm. I am supposed to loosen the reins. I know how to be and what to do. But my adrenaline spikes and I do not own my actions right now. I lean back and pull on the reins with all my might.

My hat flies off. The end of the arena approaches. In less than a second a four foot white fence will be in front of us. I pull on the inside rein with everything I've got. At the last moment she drops her inside shoulder and screams into the turn. My body leans with hers like I'm some daredevil motorcycle racer cornering the track. She comes out of the turn still at a dead run. With my wits about me now, I release my clenched grip on the reins so she will let go of her brace against them. She can't fight against something not fighting back. I release the reins and the horse's charge weakens. With nothing restraining her, Oakley relaxes. I then choke up on the inside rein and bring my hand out wide and try to take her into a circle. Her neck bends. I almost have her thought to follow the rein. If I can just circle her enough to disengage her hindquarters a bit...

Suddenly another corner is upon us. She drops her shoulder and fires into the turn. I ride through it and we come out into the straight-away running again. I have helped horses through bolting before. I knew to have great groundwork, a connection, a solid foundation in seat, leg, and rein control when riding. I knew how to spot fear in a human and a horse, and to make sure the horse was healthy and at peace with being ridden. I knew saddle fit, and knew about the rotation of the shoulder at the canter. I knew to release the reins, how to use the one-rein slow-down, and the cavalry stop.

When something needs to move out of fear it must have complete freedom to do so without restraint. Any force or pressure only creates a more threatened mind and a stronger fight. I understood bolting, why it happens, and how to move beyond it.

Yet here I was.

What did I miss?

I love horses. And now here I was on top of one hoping I didn't die. But the horse wasn't out to get me. It had no thought in its mind other than the one I had in mine: survival. Our two ultimate desires just colliding.

I relax into the ride. Little things start to come. A bend in the neck, then turning, with her inside hind leg crossing more in front of her outside one. We're getting there, she's coming back...

And then I see my hat on the ground in front of us. It innocently sits there, dusty and worn, about to play a part in the scheme of all this.

Little things.

We're turning to the right and we need to keep turning to the right. We need to go to the right of the hat, to the inside of the arena. To the left is the fence and no room. I sit deep and work the inside rein, hoping to keep her relaxed while guiding her thought to the right. The hat gets closer. I look to the right. I am all in. The hat approaches. We're headed straight for it. I look, I believe, I give all I have to the right.

She sees the hat and cuts left and rides directly into the fence. She slides to a stop and rears into the air. I come out of the saddle and land standing on the ground. She lands beside me and suddenly we are side by side looking at each other. All is quiet. I am unaware of anybody watching even though there is a crowd. Oakley stands with me and I with her. We are both wide-eyed and breathing hard, but we have survived. There's no blame in us right now, just looks of astonishment. What happened, happened.

This moment of us standing there feels longer than the ride. We both wanted the same thing, safety, we just had two different views of how to get there. But it somehow feels like we made it through together.

Was there one moment where we could have got ahead of it? One little choice we could have made differently? Can something so meaningful really be swayed by some tiny moment lodged way back in the line of things?

It would be like trying to trace a wind back to its birth. That first seed of a breeze that ever so lightly stirred a leaf. That first sign of a great storm to come. Seems carved into the stonework of existence, the big things need their little beginnings. The inevitable surprises need their first step.

"This isn't working," Calla says stoically.

I'm exasperated. I hold out my hands, palms up, in total loss. "I don't want to keep going the way we are either."

She will not look at me. She's feverishly moving around the room gathering items and putting them in her backpack. I'm afraid to ask why she's doing this.

I pivot in the middle of the room, trying to engage her. "This has to do with both of us. There's a middle here. The subject and the photographer creating the image together, right?"

She does not stop moving. "Maybe there's no picture here to be taken."

"I know we're both having our doubts. I just think there's something more here," I say.

She turns to face me. "All I am saying, is that we need to be honest about this."

"I am in complete agreement with you that something has to change."

"We're in a cycle and it's never gone away," she says. "You're not happy and I'm not happy and we keep fighting it. And I just can't do it anymore."

She continues to gather her things. A quietness comes over the room. I need to do something but there's nothing to do. I don't know what's about to happen. I know it's going to hurt, though.

I walk out the door. I make it to my car just before I start crying. I'm in so much pain.

She comes out. She's crying. She walks up to hug me. We hold the embrace for a long while, and then she steps back and looks into my eyes.

"I'm sorry. I wanted this so much," she says. "I love you, but I have to leave."

I can do nothing. There are no words. I think of what the best thing I can do is. Have courage. Find where the love is in this moment. "I love you... and I understand," I say. Letting her go.

I call Matea and we get into the car and drive without knowing where we're going. Soon we're lost. Farm fields on one side and thick forest on the other. I pull over and get out of the car. I walk out into the middle of the road and stand there. It's hard to breathe. I fall to my knees and lie down.

My hands and my left cheek feel the pavement and its rough texture. It's real, it's there, it's where I am. "I'm still alive," I say out loud.

Later in the day I return to the house. Her car is gone. I walk inside and see that her things are gone. I walk upstairs to the bedroom and look in her closet. It's empty. All of her is gone.

Matea looks up at me with sorrowful eyes. That mix of wonder and failure an animal holds in its gaze when it doesn't understand why something is.

I lie down beside her and lay my arm over her and slowly recoil into a fetal position. Stunned from the destruction of it all. Lying there bound by some invisible grasp having hold of my life. I can't get up. My mind tightens around my body like a vice, forcing me to believe that if I think hard enough, a thought will come to save me. But the silence only screams.

Matea and I go to see Rocky. I walk up to the horse and hug him.

"Is it the end?" I ask him.

The palomino looks at me and sighs, then lowers his head to continue with the grass.

I need more. I need him to be magic right now. I need to know I'll be okay. That I can trust in what has happened. That I am safe. That my love for animals is returned by them, and it will never go away. That, at least, will never leave me, right?

"Rocky... what do I do?"

He continues to eat like it's any other day. In the sound of his chewing I hear the rhythmic drawings of life. Today we live, today we die. Tomorrow we begin again, it says.

So many times I have given up on today in hopes of a better tomorrow. Tomorrow has always been there.

Until some day, that one day, when maybe it won't be.

# Chapter Seven

# The Fallen

*When I look at you, I do not see anything that needs to be saved.*

*You set forth to live, and through challenge you sometimes fall and there is pain. This is the nature of things. It could be fleeting, it could be lasting, but pain is a part of life. It is there not because you fell, it is there because it is always there. The fall just reminded you. Never forget that everything there is to feel is already inside you.*

*You are a balance of life. Sometimes this balance goes astray, usually during an experience you feel in a heavy, piercing way. Something inside tears away at the mind and digs into the heart. You stagger back and fall to your knees, glaring into the sky and shouting into the heavens, roaring in confusion, convinced there is some enemy. Why did this happen to me, you ask.*

*But no answers come.*

*So you retreat. With head low and eyes closing, you hide behind the walls you create to save yourself. You believe life has hurt you. And when you hurt, you are more apt to hurt others. The pain wants out. Under the surface it waits in agonized patience to be purged. You let it loose on others, your attack just a cloaked cry for help. A distorted reaching out into*

*the world for someone to understand. Looking for something
to fill in for your lack of love.*

*It feels like a fight to live. A rage against circumstances.
Fear tightens and festers into despair. You may even feel like
it is time to give up. A good life has eluded you; it is too hard.
You see it out there, you see what a good life is, but cannot move
toward it. So you choose to stay where you are.*

*But there is still that one thing you can rely on. The one
thing always there that holds true no matter what.*

*You are not alone.*

*There is no pain in this world that is not in another. You
are alive, connected, and that never leaves. Help is always
there. Look for it, it wants to come. Then surrender, and live
through the moment. Then do it again in the next. Because
living is enough.*

*Just hold on. There is so much you already know. So much
inside you. All the love, all the joy, all the peace... it is all there.*

*You are safe.*

*You are loved.*

*And you are never alone.*

It's fair, really. However much you love something is equal
to the pain you feel when it's gone. I suspect that's the way it's
always been and always will be.

I sit on a stump in the middle of the woods, surrounded
by a silence that sears my mind. My heart is drained dead but
somehow finds ways to continually die more.

Calla is gone.

Matea lies nearby, and will lie there as long as I sit here. She
watches and waits for signs of us moving on. I feel I'm letting

her down. She has no choice but to take on the burden of my sadness. I cry because I am sorry. I'm sorry I brought us to this.

I see no way ahead. Without Calla there's only a dark chasm of emptiness, no forward to feel. I stare off into the pine trees and think about what could have been. Sometimes I think about what I could do. Is there something I could write to her? But nothing comes, and I'm scared to death of what that means.

Matea watches over the land. She is poised and untroubled. At regular intervals she checks in with me. Her only movements are just slight turns of the head. She blends in to the fallen leaves on the forest floor. Someone could walk right by without seeing her. Her nose dances in small twitches as the smells of the land tell their tales. Her eyes widen and her body tenses with any sound no matter how small. She settles, waiting again for what comes. So content in the living of life.

The horse's name is Paden. He's a large Canadian cheval, big and black and beautiful, and very quick for his size. He's tentative and shy, something that has caused the quickness in him to be honed to perfection over his young six years. His previous owner had worked with him in a fearful way, afraid of his size and what could happen. When Paden would get anxious and nervous it would unsettle the person, causing them to try and stop it by applying more pressure and restriction to him. This only made him more fearful. All he knew was that when he got scared, he got in trouble.

Paden was well cared for, the person felt deeply for him, but the training was hard and stressful for both of them. Neither could fill in for the other. They were both just scared. The person had great love for the horse but also a great fear of him.

Soon going out to the barn happened less and less. The butter-flies in the stomach outweighing the passion in the heart.

And so this person had courage. It isn't always about getting up into the saddle; sometimes courage is knowing when to step away. The owner looked for a new home for Paden, one where he would be loved and cared for, and where his person would be confident with him.

Decisions like these can take as much heart as anything else done with a horse. It's far from giving up. If we're first and foremost dedicated to the welfare of the horse in the decisions we make, horses can be fine going to a new home.

That's how Emma and Dan met Paden. The owner felt they would be a good fit for the horse because they weren't looking for what Paden could do for them. They just wanted the horse in their lives. The riding would come if it came. And after he went home with them, they called me. And that's how I met the horse.

I walk up to Paden. It's been a little over a year since I started working with him. Emma and Dan stand beside him. I give the horse a pat on the neck. Something in the content isn't there, though. I try to come from love and connection, but it's not in me today. Patting the horse feels like going through some manual process. I have love for him and we have a con-nection, and I'm honored to be here. I'm devoted to my work and love it, but I feel like I have nothing to give. I just can't bring up the feeling.

"What are we going to do today?" asks Emma.

"Why don't you start with him," I say.

Emma begins to work with Paden in their arena. I see the love. Emma just wants to do it right for the horse. She knows he has no intent to do anything wrong, she knows he's just learned to be scared. He's a willing horse and was probably rushed in his younger years due to it. Horses like him try so hard. People can take this as confidence when seeing the horse being so agreeable. But sometimes the horse deep inside is nervous, worried, and not quite at peace with the work. The training process goes on and the horse never quite learns how to find confidence within. The horse then goes through life in constant worry when working with a human, and if it builds up too much, the horse can become very unpredictable.

Emma takes the halter off and works with Paden while he is free. He has been doing great in the work. His groundwork and connection are becoming relaxed and strong. We have been riding as well and he seems to enjoy it. But he doesn't seem to be trying today. He's just going through the motions. Emma is trying, calm in her ways, looking for Paden to stay in a steady circle around her while guiding his rhythm and gait.

He's not listening. He usually has this, he knows this. But today he's blowing it off, running around and trying to eat the little bit of grass at the edges of the fence.

"Emma, would you mind if I worked with him a bit?" I politely ask.

"Please, go right ahead," she says with a smile.

I walk into the middle of the arena with my lead rope. I feel I'm off. I know I'm off. I have no energy to fill in for this right now. No deep layers of patience stored away, no good feeling to share. I've worked many horses through this type of thing, though. It's no big deal. It'll be easy.

I begin. And the mistake is already made.

I walk to where Paden stands. His head is lowered and bent sideways to reach under the fence to get grass. I talk to him and see his ear turn to me. I softly ask him to move in the way I'm guiding. He doesn't respond. I keep asking. Nothing. I bring up my energy and still nothing. The grass is more important. I bring my energy up more, swinging the rope, and he runs to the far end of the arena. I walk to him and we repeat the process. This time I keep him running, helping him to give up on the grass. Soon we're all over the place. He knows what I want but instead keeps running zigzags all over the arena. All I would like him to do is focus on me, then do a couple complete circles around me at a walk. Easy. A simple beginning. A connection started with me in the lead, him following, and it feeling good to both of us. But his eyes are wide now. The whites of them tell me he's collapsed into old thinking. He thinks he's in trouble. The answer is no longer with me, it's now in the running.

I've had so much patience with Paden over the past year. In my mind the try is everything. It was about the journey and I didn't need anybody, horse or human, to get to any destination I had in my mind. I just wanted to help.

I just wanted to be around horses.

But it's no longer enough today. I could just stop and put the halter and lead rope on him and make it easier. We all have bad days, horses too. I could just say *lets do something else today, buddy, this isn't going as planned*. But I don't want to. I want Paden to do what he can do. So I push, again and again, more and more.

Soon the sweat is shining on his black coat.

We get a couple circles and I stop and he faces me. He's breathing heavy. He won't look at me. The grass is long gone from his mind. Survival occupies it now. I send him out again, the *every good thing has to happen twice* rule that shows it isn't a fluke. Two times or more in a row shows there's a new understanding in the horse.

I ask him to go out into a circle and he takes off. He runs with no thought of anything I'm asking him to do. I try to help him come back to the circles but when he doesn't I push harder. It isn't training anymore. Even worse, it isn't me anymore.

Everything in how I work with a horse is based on a feeling of mutual connection and the bond that develops from that. But now I'm just running a horse. He's too worried and can't think. There's no way for him to be successful.

I know I will regret this.

The frustration in me rises up. All the patience I have day after day — getting along with all the spooking, bucking, kicking, rearing, and bolting. Where was I going with all of this? Why do I have to go through the same things over and over?

Paden keeps running and I keep running. Finally I get running so fast I trip. My body flails forward trying to steady itself. Soon the struggle is lost and I dive face forward into the ground. Sand mixes with sweat and spit to plaster my face. I get a mouthful of it, and my eyes are blinded by the gritty paste.

And suddenly the frustration is gone. Nothing's left inside. It's spent in the fight and now emptied out into the regret. I roll over and lie there looking up into a cloudy sky. The air is raw. I feel it in the sting on my hands. Maybe it will rain, feels like it could.

"Are you okay?" Dan yells.

"Yes. Thank you."

He and Emma let it be.

It's so relaxing, just lying here. Giving in to it all and just letting it be. Surrendering. It is what it is.

I sit up and look to where Paden stands. He looks outside the fence. He then walks to the gate, to where Emma and Dan stand. They have put their confidence in me, trusting that what I am doing is right. Just like so many before them, putting their trust in me, all when I'm learning as I go too.

I get up and walk over to where they stand. Paden takes a cautious step back. "It's okay, boy," I say with a nod of my head, finding it hard to look at him. "It's okay."

I look to Emma and Dan. "I'm sorry. I got… caught up in something there that, well, I'm regretful about."

"Oh, it's okay," Emma says from her heart. "He was giving you a hard time."

"I let that escalate, though, when I could have just stopped at any time. There was nothing there that needed to be fixed. What happened was… he and I got lost, and instead of helping us, I just pushed harder. You can't fight a horse and win. If you win you've diminished their spirit, as well as your own. If they win, well, then they've learned how to fight and win."

"It's okay. He knows you," Dan says. "He knows you're a good guy."

I softly place my hand on Paden's withers. He lowers his head and softly blinks his eyes.

They still believe in me, humans and horse. They're filling in. They see the goodness in me even when I don't.

It wasn't just Paden that I had been fighting.

I've been fighting life for a long time.

I stand with Rocky.

"What's going to happen to me?"

He keeps eating grass. Takes a small step forward. Then another. His head softly turns back and forth over the ground. He bites and chews, repeats.

"I try so hard. So why doesn't it add up? It's not like I'm blaming anybody. I know nobody is doing anything to me."

Rock's ear bends toward me. The only sign I see he's with me. The only one I can see with my eyes.

"I just seem to be doing the same things over and over. Last time I felt like this I took off out west. But now that's not the way. There's no place to run to. It will just follow me."

I don't expect answers. I just need to say it out loud.

"Sometimes it makes me so frustrated. Just... how hard it all is, when I know, deep down, it isn't supposed to be. Right?"

Rocky raises his head and looks at me. I look him in the eyes and immediately look away. I don't know why. For so long I have been guiding what we did together, making choices on where he will live, what he will eat, and what we will do. All when he was just happy eating grass. All when he seemed to know more about a content life than I ever did.

When he was young our relationship was beautiful. It didn't have to do with anything other than what we felt when in each other's presence. I couldn't wait to see him and when I got to the barn he would whinny and come to the gate. The golden palomino and me, the luckiest guy in the world because I got to be around him, pat him, scratch him, feed him.

But I knew we had so much potential. We did amazing things, and people wanted to see it. I loved showing the freedom. How softness could be in *everything*. How it was all about *connection*. How horses could be seen as *individuals*. He wasn't just a horse. He was Rocky. And he showed that so well. But being in front of people was a little scary for us. A lot of my self-worth was caught up in what people thought of us. I was worried we wouldn't be enough.

A cloudy sky towers over us. I sit down at Rocky's feet. My knees curl to my chest, I wrap my arms tightly around them, and tears hidden behind my eyes for years burst forth.

"I am so scared."

The crying hurts. I can't breathe with it. My body is fastened into a clenched sadness. I tremble and sway back and forth, back and forth. It feels like I'm exploding through my head.

I hear padded steps behind me. Matea appears to furiously lick my face. I turn away. I cannot handle this, not now. She follows. I turn the other way. She follows. The licks increase in intensity. She's not giving up. I hide my face in my arms. I feel her nose burrowing in. I make an attempt to squeeze together more but her nose gets through and I feel her fuzzy face, I smell her glorious dog breath, and I see her beautiful eyes. I open my arms and let her in. She's made it. There she is, the dog with one blue eye and one brown, looking at me like the world is a heavenly place worth being in.

I giggle. The crying is still there but now there's laughter mixed in. I wrap my arms around her neck, and let her lick my face until she wants to stop.

"Thank you, Matea. I'm okay." I pause to catch my breath. "I just needed to do that."

Rocky, still eating, circles us in small steps, head to the ground. Is he looking at me? I can't tell. I feel like I know nothing about horses.

Why is it he seems not to notice anything that's going on with me? Does he not care? Am I just humanizing him? Why is it I feel inside he knows everything, all of it, the answers too? Why is it so hidden in his eyes, yet easy to feel?

Why is it I feel I can look at him and hear everything I ever need to know?

# Chapter Eight

# The Comet

*You get scared. If there is love, there is fear.*

*You come into the world with a life to be lived and all is possible. Questions abound, some without answer, but never without support. Never without the light and love you are given when born. With that you venture out and see things foreign and mysterious. You listen to the wind blow. You smell the air. You taste what grows. You talk to all of it, and it talks to you.*

*I only know to be in the moment. That is where I live. Always in the great joy and honor of living. Whether grazing in the rain or galloping across a field, just being alive in this world is enough.*

*But you worry so much about what happens. You worry about all you love, like it could be taken. Living wears you down. The love of life dimming, the idea of yielding to it growing. Life is not tame, not defined, not restrained in any way, and because of this you sometimes see it as hammering down upon you.*

*But inside there is something else always there.*

*An inner glow. Sometimes it shines vibrant and strong. Other times it is strained and weak. However brilliant or dull, it is not from anything ordained. There is no fate tying you to how bright an inner glow you carry. Like a candle flame igniting another, this light is simply passed to you in the beginning, binding you to itself and therefor everything. And it cannot ever be extinguished. It may flicker, it may waver, it may become very dim... but it will never go out.*

*Nor does it know any limit to how bright it can be. In the next moment is always the opportunity for it to take on more strength. It seeks all positive thought, feeling, and experience from which to expand. It is fed by magic that is available any time, any place, and without cost. It is sitting there right in front of you at all times.*

*This light within is felt by you and then the whole world. A strong life force brings up everything around it, giving and receiving as one, taking care of the world from the inside out. And the best way to take this light to a brightness it has never been? By bringing it out of a dimness of which it has never seen. The challenge naturally inspiring it and propelling it and strengthening it.*

*All it takes is the struggle to find light, for you to remember that it is always there.*

Get up.

It's hardest in the mornings. I wake and lie there and think myself into circles. What if I had said something different? What if I had done something different? What if I just can't do it?

But there's something else. Something always there. I can feel it even if I can't see it. Deep down, but still alive, trying to work its way to the surface. It waits for a chance, a little crack in the darkness. And when it gets that chance it shoots through my mind like a bright white comet.

*Get up, go out there, get out in it.*

It can't be. A happy life can't be some random thing, some game of chance only certain people win. It can't be based just on circumstances or what happens to us. It can't be.

This comet of a thought almost outweighs the two hours of lying in bed. It wants me to wake up. It wants me to get up. It wants me to let go and live. But it disappears back to the depths, swallowed by the layers of thought, and like the tail of a comet it leaves only a trace of itself in the darkness, a sparkle in a black sky, fading away.

I get up. I have to take care of Rocky and the horses.

I'm mucking out the corral near the barn. Rocky stands close by. The other horses graze out in the field. He watches me. His body is peacefully placed. He stands rooted to the ground with legs sturdy like oak and hooves settled like stone, and he watches. A slight breeze blows over us. His mane rises up and floats ghost-like. He blinks. He looks at me and with each soft open and close of his eyes I feel closer to him. I stop working and stare at the horse. He blinks again. His quietness reaches out. He watches me like he has a secret. He watches me like he has some surprise he's waiting for me to ask about.

"I'm hurting," I say.

*Okay* he answers.

"Don't you want to know why?"

He looks indifferent. *I know why.*

"You do?"

*Yes.*

"Why then?"

*Because you just told me you are.*

"Wait... what?"

*You are hurt because you just told me you are hurt.*

"Well I don't want to hurt like this, though."

*Okay.*

I stand waiting for the horse to say more. He doesn't. "What are you waiting for me to say?" I ask.

*Whatever you want.*

"I said it. I don't want to hurt anymore."

*Okay.*

Again the horse looks at me like it's up to me to say something. This time I hold fast and wait for him to speak.

He finally does. *Do you think I am supposed to save you?*

I say nothing and keep my eyes fastened to the horse.

*Because I cannot.*

The words stab into open wounds. I take a deep breath. "I know. I'm not asking you to save me," I say. "I'm not asking anyone for that. I'm just hurting, that's all, and I don't know what to do."

*This hurt you feel, will it stay forever?*

I fight the words out. "I don't know, Rock. It seems like it's always been there, way before today."

*So what you are saying, is that what caused the hurt followed you and keeps hurting you over and over again?*

"No, what I'm talking about is the... the after-effect of something that hurt. Or even a hurt that you might be... born with, or something."

*The after-effect?*

I think about how to explain this. "It's... it's in your heart."

*It hurts your heart?*

"Not your actual heart. Your feelings, your... in your mind."

*Can you get over this hurt of the heart and the feelings in your mind?*

"Well... yeah."

*How long does it take?*

"Depends."

*On what?*

"The person, how much pain they feel, and how they... go about it."

*Oh. So it could take... thirty years?*

"Believe it or not, yes."

*Three years?*

"Yes."

*Three months?*

"Sometimes."

*Three days?*

"Yes, but..."

*Three hours?*

"Maybe, if it's..."

*Three minutes?*

"Well..."

*Three seconds?*

He waits for my answer.

*Can it be done in the moment?*

I stand there staring at the horse until I have to answer. "Yes. I guess someone could get over it in the moment."

*Well do that then.*

"It's not that easy, Rock. I mean, look at horses. You guys can have a bad experience and be changed by it forever, with bucking and bolting and rearing. Things hurt us just like they do you, and we want to protect ourselves from it happening again, just like you."

*Horses can get over any of that stuff, though. You say that all the time.*

"I know."

*You also say it does not matter how long it takes, that the journey is the greatest part.*

"Yeah, I know I say that."

*You say that is where the depth of experience and heart and connection comes from and...*

"I know what I say, okay?"

*So what is the problem?*

"It's just hard."

*Okay. It is hard.*

"Oh come on. Don't do that again. I know how I think is important, that what I think about comes about. I know all that. So just... stop, okay?"

The rise in my voice causes the horse to step back.

"I'm sorry, Rock. It's just... I'm out of sorts inside. I'm more apt to get frustrated right now."

The horse steps forward to where he was.

"I know that anger is never good."

*Everything has its place.*

I think about the words he just said. I think of all the things people do when angry. "How can all the atrocities that happen in the world have their place?"

*I do not get what you are asking.*

"Man, that's just like a horse. You guys just live life standing there in the pasture without any thought to yesterday or tomorrow."

*That is not true.*

"How is that not true? Animals live solely in the moment, right?"

*We just live. Nature guides us. We learn from past living and that prepares us for the future. We just do it. We just live it.*

"You live what?"

*All of it. Grazing over the morning grass with that perfect layer of dew over it. Standing with friends, side by side, with the afternoon sun warming our backs. Resting in the cool nights, with no bugs and everything quiet.*

"Okay. But what about when there's nothing to eat and you're starving? Or your friend falls and breaks a leg? Or the nights are so cold you can't get warm? What about that stuff?"

Rocky stands stoically. It's not like he's thinking of how to answer, though. It's like he thinks I already know the answer.

*You talk about horses all the time. Look at us. Is there anything wrong with us? Is there anything wrong in nature? In the animals and the birds and the fish? Is there anything wrong in what we do? Is there anything wrong in our living? In what happens to us? Because there is starvation and dying young and freezing to death in nature. What it seems like, though, is that you are trying to fight it. It seems like you are trying to fight nature.*

"Well, what am I supposed to do? Just give up and let it all be? When I see a person or an animal getting hurt, should I just let it go because it's the nature of things?"

*What do you want to do when you see it?*

"I want to help. I want it to stop."

*Okay. Then do that.*

"But it never stops! There's so much pain and suffering in the world. And it feels like no matter how much I do, it just keeps happening, the same stuff, over and over."

*Okay.*

"I don't blame anyone. I know it's some sort of discontent inside me. Whatever triggers it, that's what I want to run away from or fight back at."

*So either you avoid all things that hurt you, or you fight the things that hurt you so they stop?*

"Yeah, that's pretty much it. I know it's not the way."

*You are seeking comfort. Just like horses. Either moving away from what is uncomfortable or trying to make it change so it is not uncomfortable anymore.*

"Exactly."

*But you cannot run from nature. Cannot fight it either.*

"I know."

*It does not make sense, running from nature or fighting it to make it change.*

"Listen, I know, I'm just saying it's hard."

*What is hard?*

"Life."

*Oh. Okay.*

"There you go again with that 'okay' stuff. That doesn't help. Just saying."

*What does not help?*

"Saying 'okay' to anything I say."

*Yes it does.*

"What?"

*It does help.*

"What do you mean?"

The horse doesn't answer. Instead he patiently stands.

I look to the ground. I then look up into the surrounding trees, still waving their leaves. "So… you're saying that whatever I say… is how the world is?"

*With horses, whatever the previous moment was, however hard or scared, the very next moment can be soft and confident. Anything can change. We are always right there with you, wherever you are. Wherever the feeling is.*

"And that means… that good and bad are always there, in any moment really. And we can choose…"

*There is only the nature of things, and it pulls one way or the other, and going with it feels good and fighting it does not.*

"How do you know which way is going with nature?"

*The feeling.*

"What feels like love? Is that what you're saying?"

*It feels like your whole body lights up.*

"The choice between love and fear. Or frustration or anger or hate. A choice between love and anything else, really. The choice that's in every moment?"

*Okay.*

"And the balance. The balance that's beyond the good and bad of things. That's where the most powerful love is, right? Beyond the good and the bad of it all. Just loving the experience. Letting life be free to just... happen."

Rocky stares at me. *Okay*, he says.

I smile. "And no matter how dark I feel, it's possible to feel the light in the very next moment. What I hate, I can love. If it's all just one thing, then I can choose every time to be in love with it. Yes?"

*Okay.*

"Nature is everything. It knows no *other*. It has no opposite. We need differences in our feelings, though. Opposites in order to experience life and to grow. An adventure that can't be won or lost, only lived. Could be one year or a hundred, but life isn't measured in years, is it?"

The horse listens.

"It's measured in the experience of it. It's measured by what's felt. And only in what I think are the darkest of times can I get to feel it the most. It's fair, life is fair. I want comfort, but challenge is where I go deeper. All the happiness and joy I want, it's not out there in what happens to me or in my circumstances. I already have it. I'm born with it, aren't I?"

He stands there watching me.

"So I guess you would tell me to slow down. To relax. It's life. I can choose to enjoy it any time I want. That all is okay. No matter what, it's gonna be okay. All I gotta do is live what's in front of me, right? By trying, I am living. By doing, I am being. By loving, I am loved. And all else is just... getting me to that. It all leads to love, so with that, everything is love. I just gotta let go each day. Let go of the pain and the heartbreak. Honor it and let it go. And even more, feel the love within it."

The horse and I stand together. The trees sway behind us. The breeze blows through the leaves, through our hair. The sun is in the sky with clouds and together they sing. Suddenly there's no place else in the world I would rather be than where I am.

"And keep an open heart. No matter what."

*Okay,* he says.

I put my arms around him. I feel the young man in me, the man once in love with horses and needing nothing from them. I let go of him and stare at the horse. His gold color, the white dapples shining through, his platinum white mane dancing in the winds. I see everything as if seeing it for the first time. The colors in the fields, the talking of the trees. All there the whole time.

I look back and the horse is grazing as if nothing ever happened.

# Chapter Nine

# Warrior Within

*Sometimes I fight. For food, for protection, for those I care for. It is unavoidable. Fighting exists, and if something exists, there is a time for it. If it is in nature, it is in all of us.*

*The fight to live is needed as much as peace. But there is also the fighting done from fear. This way of living has you fighting all the time. You feel that you never have enough, so you take from others. This always comes full circle. Your attack upon another brings the attack of others upon you.*

*There is a fighting on a different level that is above all that. A fight you cannot see, although the victor determines all you will see. All battles bow down to this one face-off, this brutal match between ancient foes: to be, or not to be. There is no greater drama than the fight within. All of it with never a winner or loser, only a participant.*

*The hope is to always be in touch with the feel of what will take you higher within. Find the fight that is from love, and then follow it, and live with what comes. There are challenges involved, but you will know when it is time. What has got you this far now just wants to take you a bit farther. Mind and body are tested. "What was" will try to hold on, while "what could be" is paid for in pain. And the only thing that will stand with you is what you have spent all your days becoming. All your thoughts, all your actions, all that brought you to who you are in that moment. An army of life standing beside you, ready to take on what is holding you back.*

*It can surely feel like a fight. A battle for what your world will be. And what will come to you someday is that if you are in this fight, you have already won.*

*And that there never was a fight in the first place.*

I walk into the woods. It's early morning. The air is cool and birds are waking. Everything is beginning.

"I'm alive," I say.

I prepare to do what will feel like battle. It isn't. I just know where my mind has been these last long days and it isn't going to let go without a fight. I'm here to make friends with the silence, and if it needs to feel like a battle, then so be it.

I kneel beside the stream that runs through the woods behind the house where I grew up. Matea posts herself beside me. I close my eyes. My shoulders relax and my posture settles. I draw in a deep breath through my nose and air pours into my body like water from a pitcher. My chest swells and my lungs expand like great wings. The breath pauses at its peak. Then at some indiscernible moment, my lips effortlessly part and the breath softly seeps out into the air from which it came, and the beginning of a stillness comes over me.

I'm hoping to sit in silence and let my thoughts go. But it's not so easy. They come, many of them. They dart back and forth like crazed hummingbirds. Calla... the future... my work... money. But none of those things have anything to do with this moment. I am sitting by a stream and breathing. That's all I want in my mind.

I inhale again, exhale again, and a little more thinking drains away.

And so the battle goes. I breathe in, breathe out, and focus on nothing but the present moment and what I am doing: sitting and breathing. But thoughts infiltrate and tear into the silence like hungry wolves into cornered prey.

I focus on my breathing. In. Out. In. Out.

I'm losing ground. I start to think and think and think, all like I do when sitting on those tree stumps. I start to feel weighed down, worried, scared. Lost.

But help comes. Reinforcements in the way of humble chatter. It's the sound of the stream. The constant sound of water softly flowing over smooth stone. There the whole time, but I am just now hearing it.

I listen. Each gurgle is specific and I'm hearing each note. Not after it, but during it. In the exact moment of perception I can hear the water in a way I've never heard it before. There is no moment of thinking about it. It's like I'm not hearing it, I'm *experiencing* it.

Breathing in, breathing out. Just breathe.

And then the air. I feel the air pass over my skin as if my skin has been tuned up in some way. An itch is like a roar. But the itch does not *itch*. I feel it, but I feel no discomfort, no need to scratch it. The itch just *is*.

The sound of the wind through the leaves of the trees.

The sound of a bird.

I'm experiencing what is happening in the present moment in a way I never have. There is no thinking about it. There is no commenting on it or labeling it or separation from it. There is nothing between the water, the itch, the wind, the bird... and me.

And with that thought I come out of it. My eyes flutter open. My body is completely relaxed. Matea is beside me. I notice I'm cold. How long have I been sitting here?

I stand and look around. The trees look different. There's something friendly in them. I smile and a short, quick giggle rises out of me. I feel child-like. And thankful. Very thankful.

I walk out of the woods with Matea in the lead. I'm fueled by some sort of quiet, some peace beyond all the back and forth of life. For some reason I can't quite fathom, all is okay as it is. Mistakes and successes feel the same. Whatever happens, happens.

At night the demons come back. I can't sleep. I roll around in bed wondering if Calla and I are truly done, how I'm going to pay bills, if I've lost my way with horses. If there is something wrong with me. Eventually I fall asleep, but I wake up in the morning with the same thoughts. I lie there with my eyes in a frozen stare.

Then the comet streaks through my sky.

*Get up. Go out there. Get out in it.*

A battle wages between the feeling I felt by the stream and the fears of *what if*.

*Get up. Go out there. Get out in it.*

But what is Calla doing right now? Was she with someone?

*Get up. Go out there. Get out in it!*

I look at Matea. She's sitting beside the bed, looking at me, worried.

"It's so hard," I say.

Her eyes go wide and her head tilts to one side, the way it does when she's trying to understand me. She places her paws on the edge of the bed and stretches up to lick my face. Soon I'm laughing.

"Okay, okay," I say through the giggles. "We'll get out in it."

I get out of bed. Matea's eyes are keen with the thought of adventure. My heart is instantly filled up on something needed, all in the glow of the dog's eyes.

"I love you, Tay Dog."

In looking into her eyes, I realize I'm feeling something already there inside me. The dog unlocks it. Everything shifts the moment I remember it. There's love. I just need to remember how to give it to myself.

—〰—

*You are loved. Remember within.*

Day after day I go to the woods and with my mind heavy I sit by the stream and breathe. Sometimes I ease into the silence; other times I can't find it. The more I try, the more I find the feel, if only for a moment. I find peace and quiet within, and I remember a love for life. Meditation is like a muscle that strengthens with exercise. And when all thinking eases away, I feel tied into the water and forest and air. Someone could walk by and notice me no more than they would the trees.

We also run. Leading the way is the Tay Dog. The forward fire that lives in Matea's blood strikes forth as she cuts through forest and leaps what's fallen. I follow, darting around trees with sure steps. We charge through rivers and the water erupts in rapture. We sprint over rock and ledge, and stride up mountains to stand on their peaks and scream into the heavens. The darkness is dispelled, the anger is laughed away, and the teeth are taken from fear.

I feel inspired. And the more I feel it, the more I want to inspire others.

I go to see my mom for no other reason than to tell her I love her. I make known how thankful I am for all she does for me. I look to how I can help my friends, whether directly or by just treating them as the beautiful people they are. Random encounters with people at gas stations and grocery stores and on the highway are chances to act from love. I can give love at any time, it's available all day, and I walk away feeling stronger, lighter, and more peaceful. And the more I act from honesty and kindness, the more those gifts come back to me.

The quiet of morning is key. Watching the sun rise is pivotal. I meditate and then go for a run, feeling my mind and body. I eat well. I crave foods that energize me, foods that taste good and also leave me feeling good. My thinking is clearer. I am aware of the power of my thoughts. At any moment I can *choose* what I think about. I have control of my mind. As I focus on my thoughts and where they take me, I become more aware of my intuition. When deciding what to do in any given moment, I feel which choice will take me to a higher place. I've been doing it with horses for years—being in the moment and letting my intuition guide me.

Day by day I sit with myself and look inside. I look at how and why I do things. More than anything, I look at how I react to the world around me. What frustrates me? What am I really mad at? Because nothing is out to get me. Whether someone loves me or hates me has more to do with them than with me. Only in how I choose to see things do I get bogged down. Hard things happen in life. Is it fate? Is it random? Unpredictable? I don't know. But I know there is *one* constant, one thing I have control over: my mind. It can change anything at any moment. The great shaper of worlds. It's time to use it as an ally. It's time to join it with my heart. It's time for all of me to work together. It's time to think the thoughts that draw to me what my heart feels for.

Love all. It begins there. Then let go. Free myself. Stop enslaving my happiness within the prison of what someone thinks about me or what's going to happen to me.

My passions are re-awakened. I realize if I write early in the morning my whole day goes well. I had gotten into the habit of feeling I could write only when everything else was done. But my passions are where I get inspired for all things. They lead the way in my love for life, so I begin with them. I write, I hike, I spend time with family and friends and animals. I play guitar in the afternoons. I strum away with only the few chords I know.

I go to beautiful places. Seeing beauty equals feeling beauty, which leads to feeling beautiful and doing beautiful things. There's an energy in the beauty of the natural world. In the towering trees, on the peaks of mountains, in the charging rivers, and at the edges of the seas I get filled up on something that's naturally there for me any time I need it. A rejuvenation that replenishes me with a natural love that inspires my steps forward on this planet.

I start to see beauty in everything. I meet strangers and see little things—the color of their eyes, the way they walk, the wrinkles in their face, how they say words—and I see the beauty of it. No matter where I am there's beauty. The sound of rain coming down, the soft lines of a wooden boat. I slow down and notice the beauty that's always there.

I begin to see. Instead of waiting for things to go my way and make me happy, I *choose* to be happy and *create* my own happiness. I let go of the eternal back-and-forthness of my mind debating whether something is good or bad. There is a world of peace beyond that. A world where I feel a peace within that guides me.

Dark thinking still invades at random times. In my car, lying in bed, when someone says something that hurts, when I have to spend money for some unforeseen reason. The circus of my mind bounces with thoughts. Gone is my energy, my smile. It seems as if beauty is gone as well but it's gone only because I stop noticing it. So I sit quietly and breathe and find patience with myself. I remember what love feels like. I remember how honesty and kindness and friendship feel so beautiful. I remember how writing and hiking and animals fill me with joy. How one moment of interaction with an animal can change my world in an instant. I remember how I feel on top of a mountain. I remember the feeling of being healthy. I remember how grateful I am for my life. And soon the comet is streaking through my sky again. And I get out of bed. I drive on. I get up off that tree stump and go out there and get out in it.

I am learning how to create the comet for myself instead of waiting for it.

There are times of sadness when I think of Calla, but I understand it for the beautiful form of love that it is. To care so deeply that it hurts, to love so powerfully that it breaks my heart. Love is tied to sadness at its core, for there are leavings and endings that will come with it. And in the end I'll say it was worth it. It's what I want, what I signed up for. The price of the ticket. So I set out to love and see how deeply I can break my heart when those endings come.

There is a gentle resolution within me. The same thoughts that broke me now just pass. It doesn't feel like I've gained anything, it's more like there's something gone. There's no resistance, just acceptance, and the choice to let go and love it all. The world hasn't changed. I haven't won. It isn't a fight.

I can't fight against something that doesn't fight.

—ɯ—

I'm driving away from a farm when I see a young woman and her horse out in a field.

They walk together far away from me. I don't know them. The woman is short with long blonde hair and wearing a dark jacket. The horse is tall and a chestnut color with a copper mane. A thoroughbred maybe. The woman and the horse walk together like they know each other. Like they have been in this field before.

They stop and the young woman faces the horse. She is saying something to it. The horse appears to listen, its posture wrapped around what's being said. The woman reaches up and softly places her hand on the horse's neck. I almost can't see her hand moving but it is. The horse stays relaxed, as if planted in place, content with no needs. The woman steps back and extends her right arm outward. The horse perks up and turns its head in that direction and begins walking that way. They are going to lunge in circles.

I pull my car over. I've seen thousands of horses lunged in a circle before and I've done it thousands of times myself with horses too numerous to count. So why I stop I don't know. But I do, and I watch.

The woman asks, and the horse moves in circles around her. They walk, then trot, then switch directions. They walk and trot in the new direction, then go back the other way. This time they canter. The horse listens, tries hard, acts playful. It moves as if enjoying the feel of a run in a field. I think I see the woman smiling, but I'm too far away to be sure. But I think I do. I feel her smiling.

They are so small to me, faraway out in the field, this person and horse. Still, there's something I see clearly even with them at a great distance. It's in them together, in what they are sharing. Just a person and a horse. Like so many millions before them. Yet so different today in how I see it.

I forget I'm a horse trainer or instructor or guide or whatever. I forget I'm anything at all and just watch them. All the labels, all the definitions, all the what-ifs, all the stories I tell myself about everything, it all slips away and I just watch a person and a horse in a field. It doesn't have to be this way or that. It just needs to be what it is without a story attached. A horse and a human together in a field.

The blonde woman stands next to the chestnut horse. She talks to it again. I think she's laughing. What they say to each other I don't know, but what the words mean, I feel. Her hand goes to the horse's forehead and she rests it there. I watch them as they stand for a moment longer then turn and walk farther into the field. They walk farther and farther away until they appear a single object in the distance, some greater single thing uniting both their souls as one.

Rocky grazes with the other horses in the rain. I stand under the overhang of the barn, watching.

I walk out into the rain and stand with him. "It's the same as you guys," I say to the palomino.

An ear shifts my way. His eyes take me in.

"It's that self-preservation instinct, isn't it?"

His back has a blanket of wetness painted over it and his yellow coat is soaked into a darker shade. Little lines of water stream over his shoulders and serpentine their way down his legs to the ground. His mane clings to his neck. He has not a care in the world. He feels like eating, so he eats.

"I believe we have it in us to naturally love, to be honest and kind and forgiving. No one more or less than another. I can see it in everybody. Everyone loves someone or something. Seven billion people; seven billion ways to love. But once we feel it, it feels the same to all, and we're united in that. Love unites us, shows us we all come from the same thing."

Rocky grazes and seems to pay me no attention. But somehow he hears.

"But that self-preservation instinct keeps us defending ourselves and putting ourselves ahead of others. It creates a separation. It's where the urge to fight against another comes from. And there's no way around that. We lie and take and steal and fight. It's in our nature. We all do those things in some way."

The rain soaks through me. Water drips from drenched strands of my hair and cascades down my cheeks. It passes over my lips and tastes so real, so important.

"I see things now about myself I didn't... or *couldn't* see while I was with Calla. I was too clenched up. But I'm beginning to understand why I do the things I do. Why I sometimes have a hard time with life. Why I react the way I do when scared."

It's there in his eyes. How he listens I do not know, but I know he hears me.

"It all had to happen."

The horse grazes while I let my thoughts come. It's always these times when they come so easy.

Standing with a horse in the rain is a beautiful thing.

# Chapter Ten

# What Goes and What Stays

*You look at the world with awe and you see the possibilities.*

*Somewhere along the way that awe may slacken and the possibilities fade. You may even come to believe you are alone. When one gives birth to multiple offspring they call them brothers and sisters. We all come from the same source, born in relation. You forget this, believing you must find something outside of yourself in order to not be alone.*

*It is instinct to seek experience, and it is instinct to seek companions. Through both you discover so much about life. Connecting with others inspires and teaches, and shows you the love in your heart. But it is not where you become not alone. It is not where that search lies, for if the place where you are not alone is outside of yourself, how can you ever truly not be alone?*

*I understand. Sometimes when I am away from my herd I do not feel safe and I cannot rest. But there is a difference between being on my own and being alone. There is safety in numbers, yes, but you can also be alone in a crowd of many. Alone is a feeling, a place in the heart. It can be felt anywhere, anytime. To understand this takes a bit of experience. Not in years but in the heart. And when those times in the heart add up just right, you remember you are not alone, nor were you ever. We are all born of the same magic, and in that we are eternally alive in each other.*

*You feel it in yourself. There lies the true beginning—feeling the love you are born with. The love that can never be taken away. The love that is always there for you to choose. It is sometimes hard to believe but you have choices and they are all yours and you can do whatever you want. And if you make choices from your heart, you get quiet inside. You soften and need less. You live from the inside out, and what is inside you creates a beautiful world outside. And so then life comes to you. Like the tail of the content cat, happiness follows wherever you roam.*

*The adventure is the fun. All the travels of the heart that lead you back to the beginning, remembering you were born into this world as part of it. Feeling at last you are never alone. Discovering what you knew all along underneath all those layers.*

*You remember we are all one.*

—₥—

So it seems I could sail the seven seas, climb the tallest mountains, learn from the greatest teachers, read thousands of books, listen to all the music, make money until money no longer matters, exercise until I'm as healthy as humanly possible, travel the world and see it all and do it all and be it all. But she'll always be there.

That look. The voice. That walk. The smile. That laugh. Those green eyes and their way of seeing the world. That heart and its way of being in the world. Everything about Calla still draws me. The attraction has not been weakened by any pain. My love for her teaches me what love for another truly is.

Why then were we in such pain? So much emotion went back and forth between us, like the tide giving and taking to the sea. It seems love wants nothing but truth and it cannot stay quiet while existing in fear. Like wind-blown trees, we weathered the storms with all our courage and we now stand naked, stripped of all leaves, with tattered limbs and scarred bark. Two trees with nothing but treeness left. Nothing but raw life showing. How much of this breaking down can we withstand? For all trees can fall. It's the nature of things.

Yet my love for her doesn't fall. It feels no lessening for the challenges. Nor does it grow. It feels the same as it always has. Dependent upon nothing. It sees nothing to lose but also nothing to gain. Whether living or dying I love her the same.

*If your heart is open to it, I would like to meet and talk*, I say in a text.

*Yes. I've been feeling that as well*, she answers.

Can we really ever change?

The young horse is naturally confident. Dancer is a paint with black and white markings and a thick mane cascading proudly around his neck. He's happy around humans, curious in life. I'm meeting him because he's been bucking people off the moment they sit on his back.

His groundwork foundation is strong. He has a deep-hearted try to do what is asked. He's healthy, moves well through his body, and carries himself with a natural balance. I palpate his back and find no signs of discomfort. I examine the saddle and how it fits. I square Dancer's feet so his back is level and see where the saddle naturally wants to settle on him. The form of the saddle matches the lines of his back. It sits level and has wither, shoulder, and spinal clearance. There's no bridging. The girth placement is correct. I gradually tighten the girth to determine whether he has a sensitive stomach area from ulcers maybe.

Any horse is uncomfortable in some way with a saddle on its back. Horses are living beings with sensitive skin and hard bone and flexing muscle, and joints that bend and twist and turn. They're also built asymmetrically, just as humans are, with subtle and sometimes major differences from one side to the other, and often develop more differences as they grow and age. Saddles are built out of, or from a combination of, wood and steel and plastic and leather. We then strap these saddles to the horse's back and tighten it around their chest and stomach area. Then we sit on it. Common sense tells us the horse will be uncomfortable in some way, it's just to what degree. This has a lot to do with the fit of the saddle as well as the sensitivity of the horse. A poor-fitting saddle has caused many a would-be willing horse to buck or rear or bolt, or to just feel a general sense of anxiety.

But the saddle fits well. Dancer shows no signs of being at odds with it. His back doesn't appear to be sore and he lets me saddle him while he's free, un-haltered. A horse in pain will typically move away from the saddle if it has the freedom to do so.

Many horses never become fully at peace with having a human on their back. It mostly has to do with how we push and force and rush it without having a feel for how the horse feels about it. It can also have to do with how they feel their body in an almost conceptual way, having areas they can't see or touch. Having a human sit on their back can feel very foreign to them.

I unsaddle him, and with a halter and lead rope on him, I move with him and help him to feel good about my guidance. His focus and try are there. I rub my hands along his back and sides. His ears are on me, and I see his eyes blinking softly. I move as if I'm going to jump up onto him bareback.

*I'm okay with that*, I hear.

I jump up and lie across Dancer's back. I breathe and stay loose and move around a bit, continuing to rub his sides with my hands. "How do you feel about carrying me?" I ask him. "Are you okay with that?" Both his ears are turned to me, he's thinking about me, and his back stays relaxed. I feel him keeping his feet steady in order to balance with me as opposed to readying his feet to get away.

I turn and lie flat along his entire back, with my head at his withers and my legs stretched over his hindquarters. I rhythmically move my hands and feet as if I'm swimming. Dust and dander rise up and coat me like a layer of paint. I see his ears still on me. He's involved, still with me. But his right eye is a little tight and he blinks less often.

We're getting close to it.

I slowly move my right hand toward his flank and he jumps. No middle ground here. His head shoots up and his body tightens like a clenched fist and he launches himself into the air. I slide off and land safely on the ground and guide his movement into a circle around me. We meet halfway: he gets to move, I get to show him how. He thinks about what to do and then slows down. I see it in his eyes that he wants to cooperate, but there's a hitch that isn't letting him.

"Okay. Easy, Dancer. Let me help you."

He slows down and quickly faces me like that position will save him. If I get emotional he will spike more, so I talk softly and keep my energy low and steady. I gently move my hands

over his body. My breathing is easy and relaxed—the great
beginning—and my thoughts are laced with the truth that I
want nothing more than to help him.

The problem is that right side.

"I'm coming up again if that's all right, Dancer." I jump up
and lie over his back. When my hand comes back to his flank
his eye tightens again, but I'm ready this time. I breathe and
slow down, retreating my hand a bit, and then easing it back to
the touchy spot. Soon the spot isn't a problem any more.

I lie with my chest over his shoulders, my stomach over his
back, and my legs over his hindquarters. My whole body goes
to work, hands and legs and breathing and talking to him. He
keeps a skeptical eye but stays with me. I sit up into the riding
position, still breathing and talking and rubbing him down. I'm
getting to know every thought in his mind while helping him
to see a world he can feel safe in. Still, he worries about that
right side. I feel his right shoulder bunching up. It's tense, and
that right eye stays frozen in hardness on me.

I slide off him to the right, helping that eye to get comfortable. I repeat the process of getting up on him and rubbing him
down and getting off, hoping to diminish his anxiety. I must
respect his comfort level and build up some shelf-life to the
trust we are developing.

We come to a point while I'm up on him when I see Dancer
thinking intently about what's happening. I softly move my
hands over him, holding the feel, talking to him and seeing him
okay, and I wait for him to decide how to react.

A moment of confidence and letting his guard down comes.
He opens up, a curiosity urging him. He hesitantly turns his
head fully to the right and looks back at me while I'm up on him.

The moment lasts a few seconds and then proves too much
for him. He goes to buck and I flow with the motion and slide

off him and move with him, letting him have his freedom, and I wait until he faces me. I smile and talk to him, and when he sees me standing there unaffected, he relaxes. Then without much wait so he doesn't make an association between bucking and a relief from stress, I jump back up on him and continue the process.

That right side. Most horses are left-eye dominant; their right eye is less sure. Dancer is worried, scared. That's all. He also has a discomfort in his right shoulder. It's more developed than the left, and it has probably caused some pinching in the past when under saddle, especially when he turns his head to the right, which would bulk up that shoulder even more.

Dancer is trapped in a perception of fear. He thinks he is looking out for himself by jumping away from what's happening, getting away before something hurts him, when hurting him is the farthest thing from my mind. That doesn't matter to him, though, because that's not how triggers work. All I have to do is mimic a situation that caused pain in the past, and he is going to jump.

Inch by inch and moment by moment I ease into his thought to jump, and I help him to control himself and open to the idea that he's okay. It doesn't matter if the threat isn't real. It's real to him. He thinks he could be hurt, maybe even die. The reality is that I want to connect with him. I have to hold to that, make sure I'm true to that. Then fill in for him, give him time, and wait for him to feel new things and think new thoughts. Horses don't count seconds, minutes, hours, days, weeks, months, or years. They know only when something feels right. That's what leads their way.

And then it happens. While I'm up on his back, he turns his head to look at me from that right eye. I feel him tense up like he's going to buck. But this time he holds himself instead.

He's got the two choices right there in front of him now: buck or relax. I let his thoughts be, let him think it through, let him make his choice. He thinks... he thinks... and then his right eye blinks. It blinks again, then again. He lowers his head. His topline relaxes. His jaw loosens, he licks and chews, and breathes. He's let go of the tension. He works through it on his insides. On a loose lead line, with no control from me, he chooses not to buck, and instead chooses to follow the feeling of what's in this moment. He gets to see what's on the other side of his fear.

Relaxation. Confidence. And me, sitting on his back, rubbing him, scratching him, and breathing all of the good thoughts. Freedom, I hope it feels to him like freedom. Freedom from the thoughts that once saved him but were now only getting in the way of new days, new living.

We end by riding around bareback. Once he's able to have me up there, being at peace with carrying someone, he breathes out deeply and lowers his head, and his eyes let go of that last bit of hardness.

Thankful for the change inside.

—⚏—

"How are you?" Calla asks.

"Good. Even though I feel like I died in some way."

"Me too," she replies.

We walk a wooded path near the ocean. At first we are protective. We wait to see where the other is going to come from. We talk of how we've been, what we've been doing. Easy things said and heard.

We come to an old tribe of trees and sit down on an orange bed of pine needles. Matea lies nearby. Our surface talk continues, our words like the needles themselves, a thin layer covering great depths. The silence settles around us, and soon inside us. The gathering of words to come. The next things said will sweep these pine needles away and burrow into those depths to find the roots of this day.

She looks into the trees. She thinks of what to say. She takes a subtle deep breath, looks me in the eyes, and says, "There's a deep love here. I feel it for you, and I know you feel it for me. But our dynamic. There's something about it that creates some sort of... friction."

"It never left us much time to rest," I say.

"No."

We sit quietly for a moment.

I speak. "The love I feel for you, Calla... it feels like a love that will get me through anything."

She listens like she always does, immersed. She then says, "I guess the question is... is love enough? No matter the pain that comes with it? No matter how hard it gets?"

We sit in silence. It's like concrete hardening around us. She looks like she could cry. I'm not sure what she believes, if she's come here to fully let me go. That may be the way, where the true courage lies. But I can't get away from the rising feeling there's another courage still left in us.

"Calla, there's a way," I say. "As long as we feel this love, there's gotta be a way we can help it. Something we can change. Something we can let go of."

"Something we surrender to."

"Yes."

She thinks. "We once talked about fate and freedom," she says. "Which do you think this is, this moment?"

"Honestly, I don't know. I don't think we *can* know. We're supposed to just live it. And right now, in this moment, I love you. It's as true as anything in the world can be. And following

that feels as right to me as anything could. So that's my truth.
That's my answer for all things. My fate *and* my freedom."

"People love each other all the time, though. It doesn't mean
they're meant to walk together for the whole way."

"There's no disagreeing with that. What matters in this
moment is where the courage is. Which is the way of love.
Not thinking about what will be scary or hurt us and moving
away from that, but feeling for what we love and finding the
way to follow that. And right now I feel my life connects to a
path with you on it."

There's desperation in her eyes. She's begging to know
something, to have an answer, to know how we can have
such problems when we love each other so. She moves with
a balance of mind and heart. She cares for her spirit and what
best serves her journey. She knows the courage to let go and
love. She also knows the pain of parting can sometimes be the
greatest love one can give oneself and another.

She speaks sincerely and says, "I feel the same. But I'm
scared... for myself and for you. I don't want to see us hurting
like we did."

"We don't have to hurt like we did. There's gotta be a way
of... letting go," I say.

"It takes huge work," she says. "When people are in a relationship they bring out each other's fears and pains, and not just
the ones on the surface, not just the ones we can easily make
sense of. Stuff comes up from unknown places burrowed deep
down, maybe even not from this life alone. Pains that hide
unhealed and direct us from some unseen sense of self-preservation. And when these pains get stirred up we lash out at the
person who agitated them. Usually a loved one. But like when
someone gets cut, the pain they feel is simply asking them to
take care of something. The pain is talking to us, showing us an

area that needs help. But we spend all our time trying to keep people from poking our wounds, when we should be focused on healing those wounds."

"Pain is a guide. A locator. It wants to help us move beyond something that hurts inside."

She nods.

"And there's a limit to the amount of stress we can feel," I continue. "We have to be aware of how much pain we're causing another and ourselves. If we keep repeating the same things over and over... something dies. It's nature. We have to grow and change, or the relationship dies off."

"I agree," she says.

Calla and I sit in the quiet of the forest for a while. I look at Matea. She seems to give life freedom to play out as it will. All with no fear.

"So much has come to light for me through this relationship," I start. "I'm able to see... me. When I stop looking at you as the cause of any pain I'm feeling, and instead see that what comes up in our romantic relationship just locates and stirs up the fear that's already inside me, then... I relax. It puts my life in my control. I realize I need to work on myself and how I see the world and react to the world. That it's not the world that hurts me."

"I've had some insights into how I live as well," she says. "I think it's important to be able to name what an issue is, to best be able to work on it."

"Facing our challenges within, changes our world and how we live in it."

"There's got to be a balance also, of helping the other by not doing the things that cause them fear and pain."

"I strongly believe that as well," I say.

"I think… it's about seeing all this in how we live," she says. "These things that hurt us, it's about noticing them when they're happening, and knowing why it happens."

"And knowing they don't define us. That they're just emotions, and every person has every emotion in them. It's being able to… learn to express our emotions, but not let them take us for a ride."

Two seagulls fly over in unison as if tied to the other by invisible strings.

"There's so much," she says as she watches the birds. "There's the never-ending, cyclical need of having the other show or prove their love. There's courage and chances and clashes. The wondering and worrying and endless what-ifs. There's insecurity, vulnerability, and the fact that the more in love, the more we can get hurt."

"That's love. It's all of that."

She sees through the future of it and says, "And it can also be easy. It can come effortlessly, with each partner looking out for the other. Asking, seeing, sensing, and knowing what their partner needs. The looks, the glances… the touches and smiles."

"Always being there."

"Dedication. Perseverance. Patience."

I smile. "And tiny kisses to cheeks in the middle of the night," I say.

We pause for a while. Our words are coming free.

"It seems when you connect your life to another person," she starts, "that it's like living with half your heart in them. That's the chance. There's the vulnerability."

"I hear you," I say. "But not if the other person *isn't* where we find the love for ourselves."

She sits there, her eyes not leaving mine. "It begins there. Loving yourself."

"*All* of yourself. Even the hard parts. And not needing someone to be responsible to fill the voids."

"And then feeling hurt by them when they don't."

"It's finding the love inside that needs nothing for it to be felt," I say.

"And we can help each other to find that," she says.

It's true. The more we drop the walls, the more we surrender, the more we allow ourselves to be vulnerable... the more love comes to us. For the love I feel for this woman right now could cover the universe.

"I'm here, and I'm with you," I say. "The honesty and courage and strength you have within you inspires me so much. And the love you have for yourself and all the world, Calla, is so beautiful."

Her eyes begin to glisten.

"All earthly relationships end at some point. But I feel there's more to our journey together," I say.

"I feel that way too. What do you feel comes next then?" she asks.

"We get out of our prisons. We choose to not hold ourselves in the past and let that create how we live now. We shed the harnesses of the stories we tell about ourselves, the myths we rely upon to defend why we react to life the way we do. It will take time, but we can do it."

"I know we can do it too," she says, inspired. "But I think we'll need help. Spiritual advisors. Therapy. We get it out and talk about it. We don't just do the things that help us stay afloat, we take action to get out of the deep water. We face our pains with courage and then do the work, every day."

"Seeing and acknowledging how we blame, or run away, or fight."

"How we try to validate ourselves by invalidating others."

"How we look for imperfections," I say. "We stop pointing our fingers."

"We do this for ourselves and the other," she says.

"And in that we can really do no wrong."

"No matter which way it goes."

I nod. "In it together... no matter which way it goes. We can treat each other with honesty and respect, no matter what."

"We'll have to be strong, and grounded. We'll need to understand how to communicate better," she says.

I speak of a simple thing, but so hard to do sometimes. "Yes, and slow down."

She nods. "And we have to respect each other's boundaries. We can't push the other where they're not ready to be."

"I'm with you," I say. "And be honest about our feelings, expressing them in respectful ways."

She pauses, closes her eyes, and reaches down deep and says, "And can we come together on one thing?"

"Tell me."

"I don't think we're broken."

I stare far into her, seeing that down-deep place she's coming from.

"I don't think anyone is," she continues. "We all have our fears and braces and hard ways. But I don't need to be fixed, you don't need to be fixed... nobody needs to be fixed to be loved. We can love each other for who we are, right here, right now."

"Calla... I hear you. Our issues and problems aren't *us*. Love isn't dependent on what we do or don't do. It isn't something that can be given and taken away. Thinking someone is broken, that feeling is just... a locator that shows us the pain or feeling of lack *inside* ourselves. The moment we point our finger at someone else, we're pointing our finger at ourselves and what's really broken."

A river un-dammed. Why block and hide our fears and pains? If we surrender to them... if we choose vulnerability and open ourselves to the core... it may be the only way to become truly unbreakable.

It starts to rain.

"We just did it, do you see?" I say. "It's out there, outside of us now, exposed, powerless."

"I feel it," she says.

"I have so much love and gratitude for you," I say.

"You help me to see the love and gratitude I have for myself," she says.

"And I just want to go through all of this, whatever it is, *with* you."

"I want to be with you through all of it too."

We hug. The rain mixes with our tears, and eases them away into the nature of all things.

# Chapter Eleven

# The Fate in Our Freedom

*Everything leads back to it. You learn to love all that leads to love. So you learn to love all and everything.*

*There is also the quest to connect with others. You will know them because they will feel right. The look they have and then the smell. The energy when they touch you. The truth they hold in their eyes. It is not without choice. You can say no. But the ones you are supposed to be with will come back around again. They are with you, and you them, all within this beautiful adventure. The galloping through the open fields and the lamenesses. The jumps over high fences and the refusals. The bucks and whinnies, the scares and nickers.*

*It may wear on you. You may think about moving on. Sometimes that is where the love is. But other times you must stay. It is plain and simple and as rooted as an oak—you are not right without that one in your life. And so you need to care for them, wherever it may lead, no matter where they go.*

*You give them your heart in all ways. Others might understand, maybe not. It does not matter. You understand and so does the one you care for. You see it when you watch them. You sense it when you touch them. You feel it when you look in their eyes, the most honest truth there is. You look out for them, you represent them, you do your best for them. Their battle-weary warrior outfitted in four layers of winter clothes you do not care the color of with a sore back you cannot remember the beginning of and you can be consoled by only one thing.*

*The look in those big brown glassy eyes.*

*And so there you are, one more in the ranks, in formation with a broken muck fork in one hand and a dirty broken-in-half carrot in the other. Ready to do battle with the rising hay costs and frozen water buckets. Ready to tackle the hidden abscesses and phantom colics. Ready to lead with respect and confidence. Ready to face the regret from yesterday, the pain in today, and the worry of tomorrow. Ready to fall in the dirt and get back up again and again. Because all hardships fade. You will not remember any of it on your death bed. You will remember only our eyes. Those big, brown, glassy eyes. Cheyenne, Faith, Max, Oakley, Paden, Dancer… you will remember them.*

*And they will remember you.*

*For in the end the relationship is enough. The connection everything. And we feel what you give. We know you are there. We see your heart.*

*And in our big, brown, glassy eyes you will see our thank-you.*

You're climbing a mountain in the dark, but you need not worry, as you only need to see enough ahead for one step at a time. The mountain accepts any means of climbing—crawling, walking, running, jumping—and after that first hard step that took so much, and after all the steps after that, after all the working, pushing, and struggling… you realize what's truly happening. The mountain is giving back in each step. You realize life *is* fair. What you give, you get. Not later, but in the moment.

But make no mistake. Life can surely feel like climbing a mountain.

Calla and I come back together and the days go on with love and laughing. We're beyond something. We feel lighter for all we've gone through, and tighter for how we've gone through it together. Hard times still come, but we're ready for them. We know where they come from. We deal with them, softly and thoroughly, and move onward. There's a safety in how we look after each other. A respect that brings strength and support. A love we trust in, no matter where it leads.

She speaks of what she needs and I speak of what I need, and we try hard for each other. Sometimes we think we are trying *too* hard. Like trying to hold onto sand in our hands by squeezing it tight, we only end up causing the sand to slip through our fingers.

We see the growth taking place within ourselves, and we support one another during it. Our relationship is peaceful, and finds a balance. But this newfound balance also begins to take us to new and unexpected places. We seem to gently drift in our own directions as we discover more about ourselves.

We seek help. We talk with people who help guide us. We speak freely of our love and pain, our pasts and challenges. We learn to understand the anger and resentment that naturally arises, and we learn ways to deal with it, and how to be respectful of each other at all times. It's work, but we devote ourselves to it. We each speak of our experience and listen to the other's, finding an in-between where we feel heard and supported. We learn how to listen without getting defensive. How to be open to anything, and hopefully threatened by nothing. We feel we have moved beyond the pains we once had.

As old challenges fade, though, room is made for new ones. We are learning so much about ourselves and each other, and we are treating each other with great love and respect. But we can't help but feel what is also happening.

There's something coming that is gently gaining momentum, like an underground river quietly winding its way to the surface. Over time it rises, drawn upward by fate, chosen by freedom. It waits until we are ready and then reveals itself. The inevitable surprise.

One morning I feel it. I look into her eyes. She feels it as well. Few words are spoken. An ending has come. Some heart-breaking quest completed. The time now is to part ways. It is real.

Lone quiet tears form in our eyes. We both just want to give love and be loved.

So much of love accidentally becomes about possession. Keeping it and having it. All the expectations, rules, and ceremony to restrain it. But the heart cannot be harnessed, and the way we're given love by another cannot be ruled over. Instead of expectations maybe there should be intentions. Instead of rules there should be respect. Instead of ceremony; surrender. Love comes with no restraints. If you fight it, there is pain. If you let it be, there's freedom.

And what's left is the human experience of it. The heart-break of living a life. The pain and the peace and the love ever-present through it all.

Days later Calla and I meet to talk of what is going to happen. We walk on a path that brings us to a small beach on a lake. The water talks to us and soon we are in it. We stand together waist deep, our bodies soaked, our hair wet and dripping, and we embrace. Our foreheads gently rest against the other's, and we close our eyes.

"Why is this so hard?" she whispers.

I wait for words. I don't know if there are any. I realize I know nothing.

"I don't know," I say.

Matea lies on the beach. Her eyes, one beautifully blue and the other beautifully brown, look out over the water.

All we know is this is where we're supposed to be right now. It's a beautiful moment. We don't know what tomorrow will bring. Maybe we shouldn't think about it. Maybe it will take care of itself.

Maybe we should trust in all that ever happens.

"Why is it so hard?"

The palomino horse grazes. I wait for an answer. A sign. Anything that speaks to me.

Rocky chews the grass like it's any other day.

Does he have the answers? Is he going to talk to me and guide me in what to do? Does God speak through him? Is it me just projecting into him what I want to hear?

"Are there any answers?"

I breathe out deeply, and sit down in the grass. I look at the dog and the horse. What is in them, who they are, Rocky and Matea... it breaks my heart and overflows it with love all at the same time. I love them so much. They are so beautiful in just who they are without doing anything to be anything. And as I sit here they tell me nothing. But in them is every answer.

There is a place beyond the good and the bad, a place where we can live beyond the pain we put ourselves through. Not the pain of heartbreak, but the pain we self-inflict. The babble in our brains that judges everything. There's a way beyond that and it can be seen in the horse and the dog. And when they show it to us, we remember the most wonderful thing—that it's in us as well. That it's all pretty simple. It's just living. It's just living the life that we've been given. In that there is a joy that rises from within and stays.

I look at Matea. Living in the moment, wise in all she has learned, and letting tomorrow come to her. I look at Rocky. His hair is getting longer. A winter coat coming in. It seems nature is looking out for him.

He's so beautiful, and he doesn't have to do anything to be beautiful. I could just sit and watch him all day and be filled up with everything I need to live. The golden palomino, Rocky, running over the open fields, living and loving a horse life.

When you have nothing left to lose, but also nothing left to gain, that's where true freedom reveals itself.

I lie back and look into the sky. What a glorious thing, to live a life. Maybe we shouldn't fight those times when we die while alive. Maybe we should trust it. Let it happen. Then choose what stays and lives on inside us.

I stand up and walk to Rocky and hug him.

"I love you, Rocky."

He lifts his head up and I hug him tightly in an attempt for our hearts to be one. I let go and he looks at me. He then goes to scratch his belly. I help him by scratching the spot for him. He raises his head into the air and wiggles his lips in joy. I laugh.

I pat him on the neck and walk back toward the barn. He lowers his head and continues grazing. I whistle for Matea and she comes running. She jogs by me and gets up ahead. The Tay Dog doing her job.

It's getting colder. Winter will be here soon. The snows will cover the lands. The cycle will continue. All with something

growing along the way, changing from what was.
It is the nature of things.

# Chapter Twelve

# The Nature of Things

*I walk out into the fields of snow, leaving a line of hard-fought tracks in my wake. Each step of my hooves is a storied task, a constant forging onward. The sky above is a canopy of tired gray. My tail blows sideways as gusts of wind lash across the land and drive the snow up and into the air in fitful bursts.*

*I come to the middle of the field and stop. Why here I do not know, but I listen to what stops me. As I stand there a change begins to happen. Everything quiets. The snow starts to glow, brighter and brighter, and soon it is blinding. It is the sun coming through the clouds and reflecting off of the snow. The warmth soaks into the hair on my back. It feels so good because of those hard-fought tracks, the canopy of gray, the heavy snow. And I cannot move because of the one great reason.*

*I am in love with it all. Before the sun came out even. For the sun was always there.*

*I cannot explain what love is. The experience of it is nothing more than that—an experience—and it cannot be won or lost, just lived. We are united in that we are all in it together, and we will all have fear together. All in the name of living.*

*Our experience takes us onto the trail of finding the feel for love in every moment. That feeling, that one great gift, we are never without it. We do not have to take it from another for it is impossible to have more than another. And though it sometimes feels like a fight to you, it is not. But if it is to be a fight, it is a fight within, and can only be won there.*

*The sun rises but someday will fall for good. All we see will die. But what we give will not. What we feel will last. What we love will never leave. Since the beginning of time the feeling of love has never grown nor diminished. Mountains crumble and seas dry up, and through it all love watches over. We grow but love does not. It is always there. There is no getting or gaining. There is only surrendering to it.*

*It is a place where we are truly immortal. Where living and dying are the same. The constant change is just nature in motion. Summer moves toward winter; winter moves toward summer. Nature moves in circles and along the way shapes, colors, and content all change while staying seamlessly tied together. A never-ending puzzle of life that always fits together perfectly. One whole. One beauty. And if life is in constant movement toward death, then death is in constant movement toward life. It is the nature of things.*

*In the end, even one day in this world is worth it. Those faced with death know this and share this message freely. It is an adventure, that is all. You wonder where it all leads but it is a place you already know. You can feel it. It is never far away. It is right there with you the whole time. In this world, lives the other world as well.*

*I stand out in the field, and the motion of the land moves from gray skies to letting the sun break through. A few stray snow flakes float down and tickle the hair and whiskers on my face. It is like heaven itself is reaching out to make contact* with the beauty that is me. The beauty of everything, is in that one little thing.

I know what love is. I cannot tell you. I can show you.

Just slow down and breathe. Feel the inhale, feel the exhale. Slow it down, ease it down, softly. Slow your life down to one breath at a time. See each breath for the life that it is. Feel the life that is in you, that is you. You are here and that is enough. You are living. That is all you have to do. Live. You will be taken care of from there.

I see you. You are walking out into the field, through the snow, coming to see me. The dog with one blue eye is with you. I see the smile on your face. From so far away I can feel it. As you get closer I feel good. I feel in you a love that requires nothing. You love me for what I am. This gives me true freedom. If you feel love, you will see me with love.

And as you walk up to me I feel you are okay. You always were and always will be and I see you remembering that. I feel your freedom. You see me with nothing asked, nothing expected. You are here to just be with me. You see me and I feel your love for me. You have remembered.

Together we share space until you speak and I listen.

"This isn't about me, Rocky," you say to me, as you look out into the fields. "This is about us."

Okay.

# THE END

# About the Story

So if you're reading this it appears you made it through with me. Thanks for that. Thank you, sincerely, for listening.

Everything in the story involving horses and dogs and personal experiences was directly from my life. I called upon times from around a ten-year span. The character of Calla, though, is a fictional creation. While based on actual experiences, I created the relationship and the words spoken in order to express my thoughts on all things love. I wished to speak of my experience in life and no one else's, with all honor and respect to everyone I have known.

So what is this book then? Fiction? Non-fiction? I don't recall where I heard it, but Stephen King was once asked why he wrote what he did. His reply? *It's what I got.* So why did I write this story? It's what I got. I started writing it in 2013, wanting to talk about the love and fear we go through in our lives. But as I hope you have gathered, the story is not *about* me. What I was feeling for was a story that was about all of us. Something we're all equally a part of.

So what is this book? I don't know. It's a book. A story. That's what I got. I also have a lot of gratitude to share, so here goes.

I would first like to thank my mother and father, Pat and David Lombard, for the love and life they have given me. They have truly been the backbone to everything me. They influenced my work with horses immensely, for they taught me the great principles of honesty, respect, and confidence. To my friends, you have been there in ways heroic to me. To my teachers, thank you for your patience and for always being there at just the right time. To those I work with and their horses, thank you for inviting me to be a part of your journey. Thank you for your trust.

A very heartfelt thank-you to Barb Foster and her keen eye during the editing process of this book. She was super insightful and encouraging, all while teaching me so much about writing. Her help with this book was monumental. Josh Libby, one of my oldest friends, helped as well with the feel of the story. "I think you should go all in on this," he said to me at just the right time.

There's a glow in Kim Graham's eye when she's behind a camera and it helps her to take amazing pictures. The front and back cover images on this book are courtesy of her, and I am so very thankful for what she captured.

There's nothing like a great foreword at the beginning of a book to set the tone. Kevin Hancock's writing did that for this story. I am eternally grateful to him for that. And Helen Peppe's blurb on the back of the book was a great final piece. Both Helen and Kevin are beautiful writers, and I urge everyone to check out Helen's book *Pigs Can't Swim* and Kevin's book *Not For Sale: Finding Center in the Land of Crazy Horse*.

Matea... the Tay Dog... has walked beside me for every laugh and every cry. She won't let me go through anything alone. Always there with all her heart and dedication, trusting in our road ahead.

To Rocky. He has one hoof in this world and one in the other. When I look into his eyes I'm okay no matter what. My heart streaks across the sky for the fact he chose me to walk this world with.

To all of us in all the world. I love you all. We're in it together. That I know as well. In the love, in the heartbreak, in the beautiful human experience of it all.

Seems it's the nature of things.

CDL
New Gloucester, Maine
January 30, 2019

# About the Author

Chris first came into contact with horses at the age of twenty-six in his home state of Maine. Within months he was inspired to go in search of learning more about horses, their nature, and the many ways of working with them. This journey would take him to the mountains of Colorado, the Hollywood Hills of California, and the wild borderlands of southern Arizona.

He returned to Maine in 2003 and set out on his own to help people and their horses, working with them in his own unique way. Chris's work now takes him all over the east coast, working with people both one-on-one and in group clinics. In 2013 he wrote *Land of the Horses: A True Story of a Lost Soul and a Life Found*, which chronicled his two-year journey in the American West. He has also written essays on horsemanship, animals, and nature for many magazines.

Chris currently lives in Maine and continues to be inspired by horses, what they show us, and the journey we take with them.

CPSIA information can be obtained
at www.ICGtesting.com
Printed in the USA
FFHW022000110619
52954585-58549FF